BEFORE WE FORGET

Before We Forget

The Guide to Personal and Collective Awakening

Aaron Scott

©2025 All Rights Reserved. No portion of this book may be reproduced, stored in a retrieval system, or transmitted in any form or by any means—electronic, mechanical, photocopy, recording, scanning, or other—except for brief quotations in critical reviews or articles without the prior permission of the author.

Published by Game Changer Publishing

Paperback ISBN: 978-1-969372-23-0

Hardcover ISBN: 978-1-969372-24-7

Digital ISBN: 978-1-969372-25-4

www.GameChangerPublishing.com

I'm grateful that you've chosen me to serve as your guide
on this path of awakening.

Our journey together extends beyond these pages.
Scan the QR code and join in shaping an awakened world.

Scan the QR Code Here:

BEFORE WE FORGET

The Guide to Personal and Collective Awakening

AARON SCOTT

Contents

Part One
The Fracture

1. The Illusion of Separation	3
2. The Sacred Distorted	15
3. The Sleep Machine	43
4. The Consumer Plague	73

Part Two
The Unraveling

5. Fearing the Truth	85
6. Keeping It Real	101
7. Mask Off	109
8. Embracing the Paradox	119
9. Words Shape Reality	129

Part Three
The Threads

10. Unleashed	141
11. The Temple Door	149
12. Parallel Structures	159
13. Awakened Sovereignty	169

Part Four
The Return

14. Living the Frequency	181
15. Embodied Mysticism	189
16. The Final Teaching	195
17. The Path Ahead	201

Before, There Was Rhythm

Before the systems,
before the cities,
before the stories that named us,
there was rhythm.

The breath.
The heartbeat.
The cycle of the seasons.

We belonged,
as threads in a vast, intelligent web of life,
moving together in reciprocity.

We didn't dominate nature.
We were nature.

We didn't fear the unknown.
We moved with it.

Somewhere along the way, the rhythm broke.
Slowly, as the world began to arrange itself around disconnection.

The systems grew.
The soul diminished.

The world called this progress,
yet many of us felt the cost.

We felt it in our bodies, overworked and unsteady.
In our relationships, strained by misalignment.
In our culture, performing progress while longing for meaning.

We felt it.

And we began to remember.
That true power does not control. It coheres.
That truth is not possessed. It is lived.
That healing is not an escape. It is a return.

This book is a map for that return.
Not to the past,
but to presence, fully embodied and awake.

Where systems serve life.
Where economy meets care.
Where you are both a seeker and a builder
of a new way of being.

So take a breath.
Step in slowly.

There is nothing to prove here.
Only something to remember.
And something deeper still.
To help rebuild.

Before We Forget, Remember

I didn't come from a spiritual background.
I didn't grow up studying mysticism or sacred texts.

I constructed my life according to every blueprint I was handed about success, purpose, and happiness.
I pushed myself to win.
To achieve what we're told will make us whole.
And I played the game well.
Professionally.
Socially.
Personally.

I contorted myself into the shape of someone who should have felt fulfilled.
But I didn't.
What I felt was an ache I couldn't name.
A dissonance that kept rising.
A sense that something about the entire structure of reality,
what we measure, worship, and pursue, was off.
Not slightly.
Fundamentally.

I broke. More than once.

And in that breaking, I had a choice.
I could either force myself back into the image the world told me I should be, or
I could turn and face the thing no one around me seemed willing to name.

I walked into the unknown.
As someone whose soul refused to participate in distortion any longer.

And I had to believe.
Blindly.
That maybe I wasn't the broken one.
Maybe the systems were.
Maybe the version of reality we've inherited is distorted.
Maybe what we call "normal" is simply what we've normalized in our disconnection.

This book is what came after I chose to embrace that unknown.
It is not a belief system.
It is not a spiritual manual.
It is a map of coherence.
Drawn from the rhythms of nature.
From pattern.
From the body.
From our systems.
From personal grief.
And from something that feels deeper than memory.

This book is what happens when we remember what life has always known
but forgot how to say.
I didn't write this as an expert.
I wrote it because I couldn't not.
Because I believe there's still time to reclaim what's true.
To live what's real.

And because the future depends on whether we can remember what was buried.
Before the soul forgets entirely.

This is that remembering.

Part One
The Fracture

Chapter 1
The Illusion of Separation

From the moment we take our first breath, we begin absorbing stories that shape our sense of reality. They are not simply told to us. They are built into the language we speak, the systems we inhabit, and the relationships we form.

One story above all becomes the framework for everything else: The story that we are separate. Separate from one another. Separate from nature. Separate from Source. Separate, even, from parts of ourselves.

This story is so deeply embedded that we rarely notice it, yet it shapes everything, from the way we structure our economies to the way we grieve a breakup. It tells us that success must come at someone else's expense. Love must be earned. Nature is a resource. Life is a competition. Our pain, a personal failure. It tells us that we are alone.

It creates a society built on survival, comparison, and fear. Empathy becomes optional, and the pain of others feels irrelevant to our own well-being.

This story gives rise to tribalism, racism, economic disparity, and war, all rooted in the idea that my survival is not your survival. We construct our identities in contrast to those around us. We design our social systems, whether economic, political, or cultural, on the premise of scarcity and hierarchy. Loneliness, alienation, and polarization are not unfortunate byproducts. They are the inevitable outcomes of a worldview that denies our shared essence.

Suffering emerges in many forms. When we no longer feel fundamentally connected, the pain of others becomes less real to us, and compassion becomes an optional choice. Others are treated as means to an end, as labor, resources, or even threats. We grow preoccupied with measuring ourselves against others, making our sense of self fragile, performative, and easily shaken.

The story that we are separate shapes how we treat the natural world, reducing living ecosystems to resources. Forests are reduced to timber, and rivers to water rights. Biodiversity loss and pollution are treated as acceptable costs of doing business. We sanctify economies that take until there is nothing left.

This story colors our understanding of life itself. Modern materialism separates consciousness from the cosmos, treating human beings as objects and meaning as myth. The sacred, the inherent value and coherence within life itself, becomes irrelevant. The soul becomes a fantasy. Healing becomes pharmaceutical, not holistic. Death becomes final, not transformational. Our bodies are treated like machines, and our emotions like errors in their code.

And in the end, there remains an emptiness that no possession or achievement can fill. We suffer not only from mental and physical illness but from spiritual hunger and the absence of connection to something greater than ourselves.

But what if this story isn't true?

What if it's not even close?

The divisions this story creates are illusions of the mind, magnified by culture, religion, and economy. In truth, there is no other. There is no out there. There is only interbeing: a seamless web of life, intelligence, and energy we have never been outside of, only asleep within.

When the illusion of separateness dissolves whether through love, meditation, sacred medicine, or crisis, people often speak of a unity beyond words. A union with life, with nature, with Source. In that unity, suffering recedes, not because pain disappears, but because the isolation around it falls away.

Human Biology and Physiology

Biology shows us that human beings are neurologically wired for connection. The presence of mirror neurons in the brain means that we not only observe each other, we also feel each other. When someone smiles at us, our brain fires as if we are smiling, too. When we see someone cry, parts of our brain light up in the same way as if we were in pain ourselves. Our nervous systems literally mirror the states of those around us.

This phenomenon, known as empathic resonance, is observable in everyday life. A baby will cry in response to another baby's distress. A group of people will start laughing uncontrollably when one person starts giggling. Our heart rates slow when we are held by someone calm. They quicken when we are in the presence of anxiety or anger. Our biology is not isolated. It is relational.

Consider this. When people are emotionally attuned, such as in deep conversation, physical closeness, or shared grief, their heartbeats and brainwaves synchronize. Scientists have measured this in couples, in parents and infants, and even in strangers immersed in rituals, music, or meditation. We do not just connect through thoughts; we connect through biorhythms.

In times of stress, being calmed through another person's grounded presence is often more effective than trying to self-regulate on our own. This is why healing, growth, and even survival are often dependent on connection. Whether in trauma therapy or group bonding, our biology responds to the presence of those who feel safe.

All of this challenges the idea that humans are primarily independent or self-contained. We are, in reality, inherently social, wired to sense, reflect, and respond to one another. Our brains and bodies are designed to exist as part of a living web of mutual influence. The science is clear: isolation hurts and connection heals.

Nature

Our interdependence with nature is equally irrefutable. The boundary between the human body and the natural world is not solid; it is porous, alive, and always in exchange. The human microbiome, the vast collection of trillions of microbes living in and on our bodies, is not just a footnote in our biology; it is essential to it. These microbes come from the soil we touch, the air we breathe, the food we eat, and our contact with other living beings.

They co-create our very experience of being alive. Microbes regulate our digestion, immune system, skin health, and even neurotransmitters, which influence mood, sleep, and cognitive function. Gut health, now widely recognized as a cornerstone of physical and mental well-being, depends on this invisible community of microbial life. In truth, many of the signals that we think come from us are co-authored by them.

To be human is to be a walking ecosystem. Biologically speaking, you are a living, breathing collaboration of human cells and microbial life, shaped by the environment in which you exist. You do not simply live on Earth. You are an expression of Earth itself.

The minerals in your bones were once dissolved in water and rock. The oxygen in your blood was released by plants and algae. The carbon in your cells was born in the heart of stars and carried through time by trees, animals, and fungi before arriving in your body. You are, at every level, made of the same elements and processes that animate the natural world.

You are not in nature as an observer. You are nature remembering itself. Every breath you take is a conversation with the trees. Every menstrual cycle moves in rhythm with the moon. Every instinct, emotion, and hunger is the echo of ancestral intelligence moving through you.

To forget this connection is to forget something essential about who and what we are. To remember it is to return to a deeper belonging, one in which healing is about reweaving ourselves into the living web we were never truly separate from.

Ecological Systems

This truth deepens further when we look at ecological systems. What once appeared to be individual organisms living independently is now recognized to be something far more interconnected and intelligent. Trees, once thought of as solitary entities, are now known to be deeply interdependent. Beneath the forest floor lies a vast network of mycorrhizal fungi forming intricate connections between the roots of trees.

Through this underground network, trees communicate. They send nutrients to young saplings and even to dying stumps to keep them alive. They warn neighboring trees of pests or diseases, prompting them to emit chemical defenses. They can sense distress and redirect resources to support their recovery. These exchanges are part of an intelligent system that prioritizes survival through cooperation rather than competition.

Forests are not simply collections of trees. They are living communities, symbiotic and responsive. Each tree is part of a greater whole, woven into a network that thrives because each part is in constant relationship with everything around it.

Your breath is part of this same story. Every inhalation you take fills your lungs with oxygen that was released by plants, trees, and algae. Every exhalation releases carbon dioxide, which these same beings use to fuel photosynthesis, the process that creates the very building blocks of life.

The cycle is seamless. There is no clear boundary between you and the forest, sky, or sea. Separation is an illusion held together by the limits of your perception. Your body is made of food grown in soil nourished by fallen leaves and rain. Your cells are powered by sunlight converted into sugar by plants. The life within you is borrowed, shared, and continuously exchanged.

Your sensory systems deepen this reciprocity. They illustrate your embeddedness in the world. Vision, sound, touch, taste, and smell are evolutionary adaptations tuned to the ecological patterns around you. They translate the light of the sun, the pressure of the wind, the scent of soil, and the taste of fruit into neural signals that inform your behavior and your very sense of being. These systems are interfaces that support the body's real-time exchange with its environment. In this way, perception is participation. The body, through its physiology, serves as a bridge between the inner self and the outer world, affirming the relational and ecological nature of life.

What we call the self is a temporary convergence of earth, water, fire, and air. Within the field of consciousness, they dance together in a pattern we recognize as ourselves. But zoom out even slightly, and you will see the invisible threads tying you to everything else. The mycelial networks in the soil mirror the neural networks in your brain, while the planet's rivers flow like the blood in your veins. The rhythm of the planet pulses through you.

When we realize this, our understanding of nature shifts from something we visit or use to something we are part of. We are participants in a vast, sacred system of reciprocity. To live in harmony is to return to ourselves more fully, with the awareness that we were never separate to begin with.

Modern Physics

Even modern physics offers insights that shatter the myth of separateness. At the most fundamental level of existence, the universe does not behave like a machine made up of isolated, independent parts. In the quantum realm, particles that were once connected continue to influence each other instantaneously, regardless of how far apart they are. This phenomenon, known as quantum entanglement, challenges the classical idea that objects can only affect one another through direct contact or proximity. It reveals that space and distance are not barriers to connection. Something deeper is at work.

One of the most visionary thinkers in modern physics, David Bohm, proposed that the world we perceive, the world of separate objects and events, is only the explicate order, the surface-level unfolding of a much deeper and more unified implicate order. According to Bohm, everything in the universe is enfolded into everything else, and what looks like fragmentation is simply the way unity reveals itself in time and space. In this view, the parts are not truly separate from one another. Instead, they are like ripples or expressions of a single, coherent field that lies beneath all of reality.

Mathematical models and quantum experiments direct us toward a universe that is fundamentally interconnected and non-local. This means that the deepest relationships within the universe do not depend on physical separation. What we call unity is simply the recognition of a deeper coherence, one that science itself reveals as the true structure of reality.

This shifts our perspective on the world and ourselves. If all things emerge from and remain within a unified field, then separation is an illusion, and connection is the baseline condition of the cosmos. Your thoughts, your body, and your life are patterns moving within a larger whole, much like waves on the surface of a single ocean.

The more deeply we look, the more we see that unity is not something we must create but something we must remember. That is, if we choose to live fully conscious in reality as it is.

Consciousness

And then there is consciousness, perhaps the most intimate and undeniable domain in which the illusion of separateness begins to dissolve. Unlike distant observations, consciousness is our direct, lived experience. It is where we meet the world and where the world meets us. In certain moments, this experience shifts in such a way that the very framework of identity and isolation begins to fall away.

In deep states of meditation, contemplative prayer, spiritual awakening, or under the guidance of plant medicines such as psilocybin, ayahuasca, or DMT, people frequently report entering a state that is best described as non-dual awareness. In this state, the boundary between self and other blurs and then vanishes altogether. The internal voice that says, *This is me*, and, *That is not me*, goes quiet. What remains is a direct and overwhelming sense of actually being all things. The air, the Earth, the stars, the people, the light, the silence, all become one field of presence.

This experience is often accompanied by a dissolution of the ego, a release of the false self, a shedding of the mental construct we mistake for our true nature. What remains is awareness itself, unbound, ungrasping, and expansive. People have described it as feeling like melting into the forest, becoming the ocean, merging with light, or simply remembering what it was like to exist without boundaries.

Importantly, these experiences are not anomalies. In fact, they appear in the mystical traditions of every major culture. In the satori of Zen Buddhism, the samadhi of yogic practice, and the fanā of Sufi Islam, each echoes the same truth that the boundary dissolves and only the union remains. In Hinduism, this is Tat Tvam Asi, "Thou art that." In Taoism, it is the flow of the Dao, which moves through all things. In early Christianity, it was the Kingdom of Heaven within. Despite vast cultural and linguistic differences, the core insight is the same. This reveals that beneath the surface of our daily individuated mind, consciousness is universal. It is the field out of which all experience arises.

When people return from these unshackled states of consciousness, they often describe the same aftermath. They experience a profound shift in perspective, a loosening of fear, and a greater sense of compassion and awe. Perhaps most significantly, they experience a quiet yet enduring sense that what they previously took to be "reality" was only the outermost layer, as if they had been looking through a keyhole at a boundless sky, but then, for a moment, the door swung open.

What was once considered mystical or metaphorical is now also being explored by science. Neuroscience, depth psychology, and consciousness studies are revealing that these states are not hallucinations but expansions of awareness, unveiling levels of perception normally filtered out by the everyday mind.

Even our language and identity, the tools we use to define ourselves, are inherited, shaped by culture, and formed in relationship. The voice inside your head speaks with words taught to you by others. The story of "me" is stitched together from collective threads. The ego, so often mistaken for the self, is in truth a social construct, a patchwork of memory, comparison, trauma, and imitation.

BEFORE WE FORGET

A New Orientation

All of this points to the truth that the perception of separateness is an illusion, a dream we inherited from our culture, our institutions, and our fear. Separateness is not real, and when we begin to awaken from it, we find a return to unity, not a loss of self.

To heal personally, collectively, and ecologically, we must return to this knowing, not as philosophy but as lived experience.

Yet here we are, living in a world built on the lie of separation. Where people die for pieces of land. Where we are instructed to access our soul through institutions. Where the success of a company might require the silent suffering of thousands.

Let me ask you something. When was the last time you looked at a stranger and felt like they were you? Not metaphorically but viscerally, like a part of your nervous system. When was the last time you looked at a tree and felt like a sibling? When was the last time you said the words "my life" and knew they didn't quite fit what you meant?

The illusion of separation is not an abstract error. It is the root of our disease. It is what makes us numb. It is what keeps us fighting ghosts. It is what allows cruelty to exist in our human-made systems and in the quiet cruelty we show ourselves.

But here's the secret: the illusion only works if we believe it. It's fragile, held together by repetition, shame, and speed, and it's constantly reinforced through media, schooling, and fear. That's how people are kept from noticing the field they're standing in.

To dismantle the illusion, we don't need to fight it or cling to some new ideology. The power to return to the real world lies within. We just need to slow down enough to feel what is true. We need to unlearn, reconnect, pause, and breathe. If we can slow down enough to experience reality itself, and live beyond the veil, we will remember.

The shift begins with something simple but radical:

A new orientation to the world, one where the boundary between self and other is porous, where difference does not metastasize into division, and where life is viewed as something we simply are.

Doorways

If the illusion of separateness is the root of our suffering, then healing begins with unlearning that illusion experientially. This process is about remembering our unity. Beneath our stories, identities, and defenses, we are already whole. What follows are doorways, living practices to help restore the felt sense of interconnection between self and other, humanity and nature, spirit and matter.

1. Return to Your Presence

The mind thrives on division. It labels, compares, narrates, and in doing so, it builds a fortress around the self. But presence crumbles that fortress. When you come into deep awareness of the present moment, through breathing or silence, the illusion begins to fade. Even a few minutes of intentional stillness each day can begin to restore the truth that reality is relational. It is whole, and you are within it.

Action: Sit in silence. Let your attention rest on your breath or the sounds around you. Do not seek insight, simply allow the moment to be complete as it is.

2. Return to Nature

You were not meant to observe nature from a distance. You are not separate from the trees, the soil, or the wind. Your very body is made of their elements. To walk barefoot on the earth, to sit beneath a tree without distraction, is not some sort of escapism. Modern life has taught you to treat nature as scenery. Awakened living asks you to treat it as family.

Action: Spend time in nature without a goal. Let the forest, the ocean, or the breeze be your teacher. Attune to the living rhythms of nature moving through you. In that recognition, you remember you belong.

3. Offer Selflessly

True service dismantles the ego. When you offer yourself to others, without seeking recognition or return, you begin to transcend the illusion that what happens to you is separate from what happens to me. Your sacred service collapses the divide between the giver and receiver. It becomes a single, seamless act of care.

Action: Perform a quiet act of generosity each week. Don't let anyone know it was you. Let your soul do the giving.

4. Soften Your Ego

The ego is a tool for navigation. But when mistaken for the whole self, it becomes a trap. It thrives on judgment, control, and defense. When you soften the ego you make space for the deeper self. The self that is uncaged, formless, and free.

Action: Journal your emotional triggers. When you feel defensive, ask yourself, *What am I protecting*? Beneath that question lies your path to healing.

5. Study Interconnected Systems

The illusion of individualism breaks down under the weight of reality. We are embedded in biological, ecological, and social networks. Our bodies are made of microbes. Our economies ripple across continents. Our actions touch those we may never meet. The more we understand systems, the more the fantasy of separateness unravels.

Action: Explore teachings on systems thinking, permaculture, regenerative economics, or indigenous science. Notice how every part reflects the whole.

Our Meditation

In the quiet, something tender begins to stir.
An ancient recognition.
A whisper beneath the noise that screams, "You were never separate."

We have lived long beneath the spell of division.
We have called it reality.
We have called it progress.
But it has been a delusion. A great forgetting.
A forgetting of the great rhythm that pulses through everything.

This unveiling dismantles the myths we carry in our minds, and even more so, in our bodies.
Now, in this stillness, you are asked to feel.
You are asked to remember.
Remember the way your breath is shared with trees.
Remember the way your body is made of the ashes of stars and ocean.
Remember the way your longing is the echo of your origin.

Let yourself rest here.
In the spaciousness that remains after illusion has loosened.
Let your own heart become the teacher now.
Let the remembering be slow, and sacred.

You were never apart.
You only believed you were.

And belief can be rewritten.

Chapter 2
The Sacred Distorted

We have been taught to live within another story that is equally narrow and numbing. A story that suggests the universe is composed of lifeless matter, that consciousness is merely a chemical glitch, and that meaning is something we impose on an otherwise empty world. But this story is not only incomplete; it is fundamentally false.

Modern science, particularly at the quantum level, continues to reveal what many ancient traditions have long understood: that beneath the visible world lies something far more mysterious and alive, a field of energy that is not chaotic but ordered and deeply intelligent.

At the most fundamental level of existence, we do not find hard particles or fixed forms. We find vibration. We find relationship. We find a vast sea of potential that seems to move in rhythm with awareness itself. This is the foundation of what spiritual traditions refer to as Source. It is not a person or a belief system. It is the living field from which all form arises and that breathes through all things.

Source is not separate from us. It is the intelligence that gives rise to stars and cells, emotions and ecosystems. It is what some mystics call the One, and what physics may refer to as the quantum field. Regardless of the name we use, the reality remains the same. We are not outside of it. We are part of it.

One of the most stunning discoveries in quantum physics is that matter changes based on observation. In other words, reality behaves differently when it is being seen. This tells us something deeply important. Consciousness is not passive but active. It participates in the unfolding of life. And if consciousness shapes reality, then our thoughts, intentions, and emotions are not just internal experiences. They are part of the creative fabric of the universe.

Neuroscience echoes this participatory nature of consciousness. Our brains do not passively record the world. They actively shape it. Perception is a construction, one filtered through attention, belief, memory, and emotional resonance. What we expect, focus on, and emotionally invest in can influence not only what we perceive, but how our neural pathways develop and reinforce themselves over time. This means that creation is not an event outside of us. It happens through the way consciousness interacts with itself, moment by moment, shaping internal patterns and external outcomes simultaneously.

We see now how we are not separate from this Source of creation. We are expressions of it. Extensions of its creativity. Agents of its unfolding. The same consciousness that births galaxies pulses in your awareness. The same field that holds potential at the quantum level responds to your focus, your feeling, and your intention. This reframes our role from passive observers in a predetermined world to active participants in an ever evolving one.

Source is the eternal flame, the origin of all energy, awareness, and becoming. We are sparks of that flame, not separate from it, but individuated expressions of its fire. A spark does not control the flame, nor does it exist without it. Yet each spark carries the full nature of fire within it, the potential to light, to transform, to create. As sparks, we burn with agency. Through our choices, attention, and alignment, we either rekindle the sacred fire or smother it beneath illusion. The flame is not steered; it is expressed. And we are how it expresses itself in form.

Creation is not a closed act completed long ago. It is a living process that continues through us.

The world we inhabit today has been shaped by the accumulated consciousness of generations, yet that evolving awareness has been diverted and distorted by the very institutions once intended to guide and protect it. It continues to unfold through the stories we choose to tell, the futures we dare to imagine, and the realities we agree to inhabit.

Engineering Disconnection

While fear of disorder or mortality may have contributed to the development of early religious structures, the institutionalization of the sacred was shaped more profoundly by deliberate efforts to centralize spiritual authority. What began as direct, communal engagement with the Divine, the living presence that animates the world and moves through all things, was gradually formalized into systems of control. Rituals became codified, sacred texts canonized, and interpretation restricted to a clerical or scholarly elite. Access to the Divine was no longer personal or intuitive, but mediated through authorized institutions.

Over time, these systems expanded beyond spiritual guidance into mechanisms of governance, reinforcing political power, social hierarchy, and economic control. The Divine was relocated, no longer present in nature, the body, or the everyday, but elevated to distant realms, accessible only through sanctioned doctrine and ritual. Dissenting voices and alternative paths were systematically suppressed to protect the legitimacy of those who claimed authority over the sacred.

This was, in truth, a strategic consolidation of power. The shift from participatory spirituality to institutional religion redefined the human relationship to the Divine, replacing direct experience with obedience, and positioning the sacred as something external, abstract, and exclusive. Reconnection begins by understanding that much of what we call religious tradition is also cultural construction. One that has shaped both belief and the very architecture of our separation from the Divine.

Systematizing Spirit

Through the centuries, humanity's innate and direct connection to the Divine, once felt through intuition, nature, embodiment, and presence, was gradually severed by the rise of institutional religions and belief systems across the globe. In ancient traditions, the Divine was not distant or abstract but intimately woven into the fabric of everyday life. The breath was sacred, the body a vessel of spirit, and the Earth a living, conscious expression of the Divine. Far from being primitive, this knowledge was deeply attuned, refined through lived experience, and encoded in cosmologies, rituals, and oral traditions that reflected a sophisticated understanding of the interconnectedness of all life. The stars were ancestral teachers. Rivers, trees, and mountains were revered as sentient family members. Ceremony was a way of staying in rhythm with the sacred pulse of the universe. These cultures recognized that the Divine was not something to be reached; it was something to be remembered. A presence ever near, mirrored in the natural world and the inner landscape alike.

As human societies grew more complex, institutional religions emerged as efforts to preserve, organize, and transmit sacred wisdom across time and space. They created ethical frameworks, communal identities, and moral codes that helped hold diverse populations together. They carried stories of justice and compassion, offered refuge in times of suffering, and seeded visions of the transcendent within collective life. In many ways, they helped anchor spiritual principles within the fabric of civilization.

But over time, these protective structures hardened. What began as vessels of transmission became containers of restriction. The ethical function of religion was overextended into systems of authority that sought to govern consciousness. Fluid spiritual truths were turned into rigid doctrines. Living mysteries were frozen into creeds. What was once a shared and intimate experience of the sacred became increasingly mediated by sanctioned authorities such as priests, castes, scholars, and prophets, who positioned themselves as exclusive intermediaries between humanity and the Divine. The sacred was externalized, institutionalized, and placed beyond reach.

This shift transformed spiritual life from inner communion to outer compliance. The original, embodied knowing passed down through songs, silence, and presence was displaced by texts, hierarchies, and laws. The soul's natural intimacy with the Divine was overshadowed, hidden beneath layers of dogma, fear, and obedience. What had once been an open field of connection became a guarded gate.

In the wake of this transformation, humanity lost its memory of how to feel the Divine from within. The wisdom was never destroyed, only silenced and forgotten. And still, even in silence, it waits.

In what follows, we will trace how this forgetting took shape across religious traditions, revealing how our sacred connection was systematically redefined, regulated, and removed.

Christianity

Christianity began as a radically inclusive movement rooted in the teachings of Jesus, who emphasized inner transformation, compassion, and an unmediated relationship with God. Early followers gathered in homes, broke bread, and shared teachings directly, without hierarchy. However, as the faith expanded and aligned with imperial power, it evolved into a formal religious structure, particularly within the Roman Catholic Church. The rise of the papacy, the codification of canon law, and the institutionalization of the sacramental system centralized authority in the hands of clergy.

Spiritual access came to depend on participation in Church-sanctioned rituals and the interpretation of scripture by ordained priests. Sacred texts were held in Latin, largely inaccessible to the general population, and religious expression outside doctrinal bounds was often met with suspicion. Figures such as Meister Eckhart and Julian of Norwich, who spoke of direct mystical communion with the Divine, were marginalized or silenced. The sacred was thus relocated from the inner life of the believer to the institutional framework of the Church, transforming spiritual immediacy into mediated obedience.

Islam

In its earliest revelations, Islam emphasized a deeply personal and intimate relationship with the Divine. The Qur'an described God as nearer than one's own jugular vein, and the Prophet Muhammad's life modeled a dynamic spiritual practice grounded in justice, prayer, and moral clarity. But following the Prophet's death, Islam underwent increasing formalization. Schools of jurisprudence, known as madhahib, emerged to interpret divine law, and a class of religious scholars, known as ulama, became institutional gatekeepers of spiritual and legal authority.

While these structures aimed to preserve the faith's integrity, they gradually overshadowed the direct, experiential relationship between the individual and God. In many regions, Islamic life came to be defined by external compliance with legal codes, and personal spiritual engagement, especially when unmediated by scholars, was viewed as unorthodox or even dangerous. The sacred, once accessed through the heart and through prayer, became increasingly filtered through institutional doctrine, creating layers between the seeker and Source.

Judaism

After the destruction of the Second Temple in 70 CE, Judaism transformed from a religion centered on temple worship and priestly rituals into one structured around rabbinic authority and legal scholarship. With the loss of the physical center of worship, rabbis assumed leadership roles, compiling the Mishnah, Talmud, and later codes of Halakha, or Jewish law, that governed every aspect of daily life.

The Divine, once encountered through the rituals of the Temple and the felt presence of the Shekhinah, became increasingly conceptualized through legal interpretation and textual analysis. Spiritual connection now depended on understanding and observing complex laws, often mediated by trained scholars, making experiential or intuitive communion with the sacred more peripheral. While this structure preserved Jewish identity through centuries of diaspora, it also rendered access to the Divine contingent on rabbinic authority. Kabbalah offered an alternative mystical framework, but it remained largely esoteric and marginal.

Hinduism

In its ancient Vedic form, Hinduism developed as a complex ritual system maintained by the Brahmin priesthood, who held exclusive authority over Sanskrit scriptures and sacrificial rites. Spiritual access was intricately tied to caste hierarchy, with the Brahmins serving as custodians of sacred knowledge and gatekeepers of ritual practice.

Participation in the spiritual life of the community, particularly access to Vedic chants, temple rites, and scriptural study, was largely restricted to upper castes. Shudras and Dalits were often excluded entirely. The Divine became enshrined in ritual precision and inherited privilege, rather than in universal accessibility. The emphasis on external purity, lineage, and prescribed roles formalized spiritual hierarchy and distanced the average person from direct engagement with the sacred. The soul's journey toward the Divine was bound by social position and priestly mediation, reducing divinity to a stratified system rather than an innate presence within all beings.

Buddhism

Although founded on the Buddha's direct realization of truth and his teaching of a path open to all, Buddhism soon developed elaborate monastic institutions and philosophical systems. In both Theravāda and Mahāyāna traditions, monastic life gradually became the primary setting in which the pursuit of enlightenment was emphasized.

The sacred path gradually came to be associated with renunciation, scholarly study, and observance of monastic codes known as the Vinaya. Lay practitioners were encouraged to accumulate merit by supporting monastics, but their own access to awakening was often viewed as deferred or limited. Over time, the teachings became highly systematized, and in some cases, removed from the simple immediacy of the Buddha's original insight. The result was a religious structure that formalized the path to enlightenment, shifting the focus from direct realization to a structured, text-based journey guided by tradition.

Taoism

Rooted in the mystical insights of the Tao Te Ching and the Zhuangzi, Taoism originally emphasized harmony with the Tao, the ineffable and ever-present flow of life. Early Taoism taught that spiritual alignment came through simplicity, stillness, and effortless action, or wu wei, with the Tao accessible to all who attuned themselves to the rhythms of nature and inner peace. However, as Taoism evolved, especially under the Han dynasty, it became intertwined with imperial systems.

This resulted in the rise of Religious Taoism, known as Daojiao, which featured elaborate rituals, alchemical practices, and a priestly hierarchy. Access to spiritual knowledge became the domain of initiates and ordained priests, and the Tao was interpreted through cosmological systems and ritual obligations. As Taoism became more institutionalized, aspects of its original spontaneity and direct insight were gradually shaped into structured practices, reflecting some of the very forms it once sought to transcend.

Distorting the Sacred

As civilizations grew more complex, early spiritual expressions, once fluid, embodied, and intimately attuned to the rhythms of the human experience and Earth, began to be systematized. What was once experienced directly was ritualized, and what was held communally was centralized. At first, this may have served to anchor the sacred within the structures of emerging societies, but beneath this practical shift, we lost the recognition of the Divine as a living intelligence expressed through sacred polarity.

This Divine intelligence does not manifest through uniformity or stillness, but rather through polarity, the creative tension of interdependent opposites. From light and shadow to expansion and contraction, from emptiness to form, all of creation moves within this rhythm. It is sacred reciprocity, a dance of contrast through which consciousness becomes visible. Just as magnetism, electricity, and even biological life rely on the interplay of complementary forces, so too does the soul unfold through the sacred dance of difference.

We see this rhythm throughout the natural world: in the breath, where the inhale receives and the exhale releases; in the nervous system, where parasympathetic stillness and sympathetic activation maintain equilibrium; in reproduction, where the masculine and feminine unite to create life. These examples illustrate the divine mechanism through which balance, natural order, and life arise.

These polarities are expressions of Source itself, the movements of Divine intelligence shaping reality through rhythm. It is from this cosmic dance that the foundational qualities we now name as the Feminine and Masculine principles first emerged. They were once held as equally sacred, co-arising and mutually necessary, forming the spiritual architecture of both the cosmos and the soul.

But over time, something more than forgetting occurred. As institutional religions took shape, the sacred balance that once honored both Feminine and Masculine aspects of the Divine was intentionally dismantled. Across traditions, the Feminine was gradually removed from the heart of religious life. Goddesses who once embodied creation, wisdom, and love were erased, demoted, or demonized. Myths were rewritten to place masculine authority at the center. Temples once devoted to feminine divinity were rededicated, and rituals that honored her presence were banned or absorbed into new patriarchal frameworks.

The Feminine principle, long revered as the presence of intuition, mystery, sensual wisdom, and the immanent Divine, was cast as dangerous, irrational, or impure. Her symbols became taboos. Her sacred functions were transferred to male priests, prophets, or scribes. And those who carried her legacy, priestesses, healers, midwives, and mystics, were discredited, persecuted, or erased from sacred history.

This was an orchestrated reordering of spiritual life. The Divine was redefined in exclusively masculine terms, rendered abstract, hierarchical, and remote. The inner current of direct knowing was replaced by outer intermediaries. The Earth gradually lost its recognition as an expression of the

Divine, the body came to be viewed with caution or control, and the inner voice was increasingly overlooked or questioned as unreliable. The exile of the Feminine from religion marked a deeper rupture in human consciousness; a cosmic forgetting of the relational, embodied, and cyclical nature of life itself. What was once an integrated dance of polarities became a lopsided order rooted in control and disconnection.

To trace this lineage is to understand that the severing of humanity from the Divine was both spiritual and structural. When the Feminine was removed from religious life, a vacuum emerged where intimacy, receptivity, and embodied wisdom had once flourished. Into this hollow stepped institutions that carried the appearance of spiritual authority while obscuring the very essence they claimed to preserve. In doing so, many followers were led to mistake their self-imposed control for devotion, and structure for spirit.

To awaken and return is to restore the inner alignment that makes true unity with the Divine possible. It is to reawaken the sacred Feminine within and around us, and to remember that the Divine has never been singular, distant, or abstract. It is living, relational, and always seeking reunion through balance.

In what follows, we will turn to the world's major religious traditions to examine how this suppression unfolded across belief systems, and how each contributed to the erasure of the sacred Feminine in their own ways.

Christianity

In the early centuries after Jesus, Christianity was diverse and decentralized. Women led communities, taught, and were seen as spiritual equals. In many Gnostic texts, Mary Magdalene is portrayed as Jesus's closest disciple and a bearer of profound wisdom.

But in the fourth century, everything changed. Emperor Constantine adopted Christianity and convened the Council of Nicaea. Christianity became the official religion of the Roman Empire. Doctrine was locked in. Mystical texts were banned. Church leadership was placed solely in male hands. Mary Magdalene was rewritten as a prostitute. The Gnostic gospels, which emphasized direct communion and the Sacred Feminine, were declared heresy. Sophia, once a name for divine wisdom, was quietly removed from theology.

Eve's story, originally a complex turning point in the Hebrew tradition, was recast in Christian theology as the origin of sin and the fall of humanity. She became not only the first woman, but the first failure. This reinterpretation fueled the belief that women were spiritually inferior and morally dangerous. Female wisdom was feared, and female sexuality framed as temptation. Eve's image was weaponized to justify the control and subjugation of women.

Islam

In the seventh century, Prophet Muhammad broke many taboos, marrying a powerful woman, Khadijah, permitting women to inherit property, and allowing them to participate in public and spiritual life. Aisha, one of his wives, transmitted over two thousand hadiths and led troops in battle.

But after Muhammad's death, Islam quickly became political. The Caliphates, particularly the Umayyads and Abbasids, transformed the faith into an imperial ideology. Religious scholars known as Ulama interpreted the Qur'an through patriarchal lenses, and restrictions on women's education, mobility, and dress intensified.

Sufism preserved some feminine symbolism, like the Beloved as a divine archetype, but mainstream Islamic practice became deeply male-dominated.

Judaism

Early Hebrew religion was not purely monotheistic. Archaeological and textual evidence suggests the worship of Asherah, a goddess and consort of Yahweh. She was venerated alongside male deities in many household shrines.

But by the time of the Babylonian Exile in the sixth century BCE, Jewish leaders sought to purify and centralize their faith. This led to the Torah's codification, a crackdown on "idolatry," and a priestly caste that controlled access to the Divine. Asherah was scrubbed from memory.

Women prophets and judges, like Deborah, became outliers in a male-dominated religious structure. The Talmudic period formalized this exclusion, reducing the roles of women in both temple life and study.

Hinduism

Hinduism is rich in goddesses, from the warrior goddess Durga to the cosmic goddess Kali. But the Brahminical system, which began consolidating power during the late Vedic period around 500 BCE, ensured that real world spiritual authority remained with male priests.

Texts like the Manusmriti codified the role of women as dependent on fathers and husbands. Despite the worship of powerful goddesses, female gurus and priests were rare. The Bhakti and Tantric movements offered some freedom but were often sidelined or eventually subsumed by orthodoxy.

Buddhism

The Buddha allowed women to become nuns, but with more rules than monks and an explicit claim that women's enlightenment would always be second-tier. This began a tradition where, over centuries, Bhikkhuni ordination was suppressed or banned in Theravāda and Tibetan traditions.

Despite the presence of female Buddhas and Bodhisattvas in Mahāyāna and Vajrayāna schools like Tara, leadership remained firmly in male hands. Tibetan Buddhism, in particular, preserved patriarchal teacher-student lines and continues to marginalize women's roles.

Taoism

Yin, reinterpreted, shifted classical Taoism, which once honored the yin-yang balance and revered the Feminine as essential to cosmic order. But under Han dynasty institutionalization, Taoism became more structured and patriarchal. Taoist priesthoods were largely male, and female alchemists or shamans were demoted to folklore.

Yin, once seen as powerful and creative, was reinterpreted as passive, submissive, and secondary to yang. Confucian values merged with Taoist texts, further solidifying gender hierarchies.

Masculinity Overextended

The Sacred Masculine, in its uncorrupted form, is not about dominance or hierarchy. It is the force of protection, clarity, direction, integrity, and generative structure. It holds space for emergence. It embodies right action in the service of life. It creates boundaries that protect rather than control.

But as power structures formed around hierarchy, conquest, and the need for control, this original essence was gradually overextended. Under empire, the Masculine became a symbol of imperial authority. The teacher became an enforcer. The guide became a gatekeeper. The protector became a patriarch. The Masculine, once in service to the whole, was elevated as the whole.

This distortion became the foundation for modern institutions and shaped the contours of the modern world itself. Most of today's systems carry the imprint of this overextended Masculine principle:

- Education centers on obedience rather than awakening.
- Medicine is mechanistic and disconnected from the body's intelligence.
- Governance is self-serving rather than protective.
- Economy values growth and accumulation over balance and reciprocity.
- Spirituality is performance and power rather than presence and empowerment.

Across these structures, the Sacred Masculine's original role of leadership through care was replaced with control. We were left with systems that claim to protect us, yet in practice disconnect us from our bodies, our souls, and one another.

This gave rise to both a structural and a psychological shift, and as these patterns deepened, trauma began to accumulate. The mind split from the body. Logic no longer walked alongside emotion. Spirit was no longer something we experienced directly but something abstract and external. The Sacred Feminine faded from view. We lost our tenderness. We lost the Divine balance in our lives.

What follows are three of the most dominant systems, each showing how the sacred was removed and distorted. We come to see that these are not merely institutional problems but spiritual consequences that shape our collective consciousness and spill over into our individual lives.

Education

A child's way of learning is wild and sacred. It is not linear. It unfolds through play, curiosity, mimicry, and connection. Learning occurs through the senses, through rhythm, and through relationships. The young mind does not segment the world into digestible subjects. It experiences life as one living field, full of questions and discovery.

In this natural state, education emerges. It is a process of drawing forth what is already alive. The body moves. The heart feels. The child explores to understand who they are and how the world works.

But modern schooling was not built on this sacred rhythm. It was shaped by the Industrial Age, designed for efficiency and uniformity. The widely adopted Prussian model, created to produce obedient soldiers and compliant workers, became the blueprint for mass education throughout the world.

Today, this model rewards memorization, suppresses originality, and replaces intrinsic curiosity with external validation. The question is no longer, *Who are you becoming?* Instead, it is, *How can you be useful?* Not to the soul but to the industrial machine.

The child is trained to obey the schedule, follow the rules, and measure their worth by numbers. Gold stars, test scores, and achievement charts are the currency of value. Learning becomes a transaction. Feeling becomes a distraction. The body, once central to knowing, is told to sit still. This system explicitly conditions children to turn away from the sacred.

In North America, the damage deepened with the establishment of residential schools. Indigenous children were taken from their families and stripped of their languages, rituals, and ancestral names. These institutions colonized. They severed the bonds between child and land, between culture and spirit, between memory and identity. They erased ways of being.

Within our current paradigm, the Feminine is pushed to the margins. Emotion becomes disruption. Intuition becomes defiance. Creativity becomes a side subject. The arts, movement, and imagination, all once vital expressions of intelligence, are made optional or eliminated entirely. Education becomes estranged from the soul.

Instead of nurturing what is already present, it manages potential like a resource to be extracted. The dreamer's passion is diagnosed. The questioner is silenced. The embodied child is medicated. In doing so, we train generations to live from the outside in.

The damage has been quiet but profound. A child whose inner knowing is dismissed will eventually outsource their truth, choosing approval and instruction over their own authenticity. In time, they learn to distrust their feelings, suppress their intuition, and live as if divided from themselves.

This is, in truth, a spiritual problem because the cost is the severing of our deep connection to the Divine within. The sacred remains unnamed, then unnoticed, and ultimately unknown.

Healthcare

Healing was once a sacred relationship, an intimate exchange between the body and the Earth, where the body itself was trusted as the original healer. After all, a cut weaves itself closed, a fever rises to burn away infection, and a bone, given time and rest, will knit itself whole again. Beyond this, healing arose through listening deeply to the full message carried by illness. Health was understood as harmony between the inner and outer worlds.

In this way, healing began in food, in stories, and in the hands of midwives. The womb was honored and the nervous system was trusted as a compass. Plants were viewed as living medicine and illness was understood as part of a larger web of causes, histories, and unmet truths.

Over time, this sacred approach was dismantled. As empires expanded and industrial frameworks hardened, healing was absorbed into systems of power. It became clinical, categorical, and mechanized. The healer turned into a technician and the body into a machine.

Women, who had long carried relational knowledge through birth work, herbs, and communal care, were targeted. Across Europe and North America, witch trials acted as a systemic erasure of the Feminine lineages that held Earth-based and cyclical intelligence. Their removal cleared the path for male-dominated hierarchies to redefine medicine.

By the early twentieth century, medical knowledge had been fully institutionalized. Reports such as the Flexner Report reshaped medical education to exclude holistic and spiritual models. Practices outside the emerging scientific orthodoxy, including psychedelic therapies, herbal medicine, and energy-based traditions, were outlawed or pathologized.

This was more than a change in tools. It was a shift in worldview. The body was treated as a specimen, and the act of healing was reduced to the efficient restoration of function. In the process, medicine lost its memory of the soul.

Economy

In ancestral cultures, the economy moved as a rhythm. Exchange was rooted in relationship. Value was measured in care, continuity, and trust. Wealth flowed in balance, sustained through the act of giving and receiving. Giving sustained harmony, while receiving honored the gift.

This was divine intelligent design. Communities found abundance in interdependence, where elders carried wisdom into the lineage, where the land gave to those who honored its seasons, and where labor became an offering to life itself.

Over time, this spiritual ecosystem was dismantled. The economy was abstracted from ecological intelligence, and exchange was detached from care. The rhythm of reciprocity was replaced with the logic of extraction.

In England, the Enclosure Acts transformed communal lands into private property, uprooting lifeways that had been shaped by community cooperation. What had been held in common was fenced, taxed, and sold. This pattern extended globally through colonization, where entire cultures rooted in reciprocity, ceremony, and mutual belonging were dismantled and replaced with markets designed to dominate.

The change was more than structural. It was a rupture in meaning and values.

The Feminine current of sufficiency, was recast as laziness or a lack of ambition. The slow, relational work of caring for life, tending to children, elders, or the land, was completely devalued. In the aftermath, growth was elevated as god, manufactured scarcity was established as the engine, and consumption became the measure of worth.

Exchange turned into a machinery of depletion, where forests, bodies, time, and attention were all fed into the fire of progress, repackaged as goods, and sold back in fragments.

In this forgetting, the economy lost its soul. It no longer focused on what is needed to live a nourished, whole life. It asked only what could be monetized. Profit replaced meaning, sufficiency was shamed, and growth without end was treated as destiny, no matter the consequences.

This economic model grew out of a worldview already unbalanced, one that confused greed and domination with success. Its tenets continue to shape our guideposts and define our economic consciousness today.

Performing Life

Across all sectors, one pattern repeats itself. A subtle distortion creeps in through policies, platforms, and polished smiles. What was once relational becomes transactional. The trust, care, and presence that once lived naturally between people have been transformed exclusively into things to be negotiated, priced, and earned.

In this model, you are deemed a respected member of society when you prove your ability to extract maximum profit from the marketplace of your profession. This becomes our measuring stick, and it is treated as normal, when in truth it is deeply distorted.

Our social life morphs into content, and friendship turns into branding partnerships. Belonging is about showing off. Experiences are curated, filtered, and posted. When we used to connect, we now advertise connection, and measure it by engagement and reach.

In the workforce, your contribution defines your identity. The question is no longer "What do you love?" but "What do you do, how much do you produce, and for whom?" We call burnout ambition, we praise exhaustion as commitment. Rest too much and you risk irrelevance; slow down and you risk falling behind. Personally, you lose the right to be messy, and worse, the right to fail. It's not that people lack ambition or refuse to follow their dreams. It's that pursuing them puts survival at risk.

Even spirituality is not spared. The sacred is sanitized, and mysticism is merchandised. Healing is broken down into clickable fragments. Peace is sold as a commodity, and meditation is marketed as a means of self-improvement. The sacred becomes something to outsource. The system fragments it, strips it of depth, and sells it back in pieces.

All of this is labeled progress, optimization, and empowerment. Yet what we lose in the process is profound. We lose the sanctity of everything. Nothing holds meaning. Everything becomes an extension of the industrial hand of monetization. Without realizing it, we are systematically removing the very space required for the sacred to resurface.

If across the globe we understood how intricately we are connected to the true nature of the Divine and how connected we are to one another, do you think we would consciously allow society to operate as it does? Would we be less susceptible to manipulation? Would we be as hypnotized as we are by external gratification? These are not questions to merely consider intellectually; they are to be felt and contemplated with the soul.

Our collective actions hollow out the soul of civilization. The more we perform and sell ourselves, the more we disconnect from one another and drift from the Divine order that orients us in the universe. What starts as adaptation turns into amnesia, and that amnesia slowly erodes everything we hold sacred.

The Real Life Hack

Amid our disconnection, a quiet invitation calls us to remember. It urges us to turn inward and reorient ourselves to the holy order that has never disappeared, only become obscured. The Divine fills everything. It lives in the structure of reality itself. It pulses through repeating patterns, the rhythm of breath, the cycle of seasons, the spiral of galaxies. The sacred is the shape life takes when it moves in coherence.

This is living architecture, a correspondence written into existence: "As within, so without; as above, so below." Sacred rhythms form vibrational fields, and we tune to them whenever we embody anger or joy, whenever we honor the polarities that shape our actions. What stirs in human beings stirs in the Earth. What forms the Earth also forms the stars.

Our heartbeat contracts and releases in the same rhythm as the ocean's tides and the universe's expansion. Our circadian rhythms rise and fall with light and dark, just as plants open to the sun and close to the night. Our brainwaves, delta, theta, alpha, beta, gamma, resonate with the electromagnetic frequencies of the Earth, including the Schumann resonance and the quantum fields beneath matter. Our DNA spirals as sunflowers, pinecones, hurricanes, and galaxies spiral. The menstrual cycle echoes the lunar cycle, linking human fertility with the gravitational and photonic rhythms of the moon.

The systems that govern modern life break these rhythms. Whether by historical design, industrial momentum, or cultural inertia, they force us into schedules, alarms, and metrics. They push us to ignore the body's signals, to override rest with urgency, to mistake speed for progress, and repetition for vitality.

These systems demand linearity while life moves in cycles. They demand uniformity while life grows in fractals. They demand control while life thrives in relationships. They scatter our attention, sever our belonging, and estrange us from the patterns that could restore our inner alignment. We live as though separate from the field that sustains us, and we forget that we are the field expressed in human form.

These systems are not neutral. They shape how we view our time, our body, and our worth. They train us to ignore the sacred rhythms inside us, and then they call that inversion normal. Generations pass it on without question.

When we slow down and realign with the rhythms within our own body, our planet, and Divine intelligence, we catch a tailwind. We begin to move with the current of Source instead of against it. Realignment is more than a biological adjustment. It is a way of living in integrity with who we truly are. It means choosing work, relationships, timing, and expression that grow from internal alignment rather than external resistance. When we honor this bond, life changes from the inside out.

Alignment with Source requires alignment with self, because we have never been separate. We are both the wave and the ocean.

Consider cortisol. It peaks in the morning to sharpen alertness and declines at night to allow rest. When we push against this rhythm, staying awake into the night for productivity or stimulation, we create systemic stress that drains our energy, weakens immunity, and clouds the mind. When we rise with light, focus in peak hours, and rest after dark, we experience clarity, vitality, and balance without doing more. Effort burns energy. Attunement receives it.

Ignoring these rhythms fractures us. It begins with small cracks. We experience dissatisfaction at work, fatigue that appears to come out of nowhere, and disconnection from our bodies and personal dreams. Over time, the fracture deepens into burnout, anxiety, depression, and a life that no longer feels like our own.

Think of a person with a creative impulse to write, build, care, or teach who takes a job only for financial survival. Each day they silence their inner pull. They wake with dread, medicate to stay alert, scroll at night to numb themselves, and cling to weekends that vanish too quickly. Outwardly they function, but inside tension builds between their true self and their daily life.

Or think of a student who dreams of studying healing, language, or ecology but chooses finance or tech for upward mobility. They rationalize that they can always return later, that this is success, that this is what their family expects. Yet their soul's rhythm bends to outside pressure. They may thrive materially, but they have sacrificed their inner alignment at the altar of market logic.

This is not just stress. It is the redirection of life force. When we reduce work to survival and treat passion as impractical, we fracture. We fall out of sync with our body, our emotions, and the intelligence that organizes life itself. Sacred rhythm is the compass that tells us when something is true. Ignoring it costs us coherence. It costs us our truth.

Trusting this compass changes everything. When we let our deepest creative self lead, our lives feel meaningful and our dreams take shape. Not because we grind harder, but because we align with the way the universe already moves, with coherence, efficiency, and reciprocity.

Following passion is not some fantasy. It resonates with the deeper order. True desire signals where life wants to flow with the least resistance. It is efficient because it is true. It is sustainable because it belongs to you.

Chasing external achievement while abandoning dreams leaves us struggling endlessly. Living in integrity with what lights us up opens doors. Resources appear. Energy aligned with truth does not meet the resistance born of self-betrayal or a devotion to illusion. It compounds, it attracts, it creates.

This is sacred physics. The soul is efficient. The soul is a guide. Trust it, and survival gives way to creation. This creation becomes your sovereignty.

The irony deepens when we justify personal misalignment as a sacrifice for our children. We claim to work hard for their better life, yet in abandoning our own compass we model disconnection. Chronic self-abandonment does not yield security. It passes on fragmentation. Through our actions we teach children that success requires sacrificing presence, that love is secondary to utility, and that self-betrayal is noble.

What is a better life if it offers more money but less meaning and joy? Children need an example of living in rhythm with their individual truth.

Because this detachment has been rewarded and praised for generations, it passes on like inheritance. It becomes a lineage of sleepwalking until someone stops, listens inward, and chooses differently. Not perfectly, but consciously. In rhythm. In coherence. In a conscious refusal to live life unconsciously.

You do not need to add anything to yourself. You only need to remember who you are. The separateness you were taught is a trance. You are waking from it. Each act of presence, stillness, service, and love dissolves the lie. What remains is everything you have been searching for all along.

Our Current Existential Crisis

When sacred distortion becomes the default setting of our lives, the cost extends far beyond the internal. It echoes through our relationships, our systems, and the planet itself. We lose access to inner balance, shared reciprocity, and the vitality of nature. The world grows disconnected, mechanized, and linear. It feels less like a living presence and more like a collection of problems to solve or resources to extract.

Human experience then narrows into loneliness, anxiety, and spiritual hollowness. This is the root of the existential crisis. Sacred balance is not abstract. It was once how we participated in the living web of existence. It is still how the cosmos moves and how nature functions. Humanity, however, has sanctified a false divinity built on synthetic logic, disconnected from the Divine order. This artificial order manufactures control and seeks to override the organic rhythms of life both around us and within us. Under its influence, we lose orientation, we disconnect, and we suffer.

The structures we created to serve industry, empire, and capital no longer align with life. They override it. These systems fracture the rhythms of the

BEFORE WE FORGET

Earth and the coherence of our bodies. Our inner compass spins without direction, and we drift.

The Sacred Feminine is the gateway to depth and meaning. Love, intimacy, beauty, awe, grief, and creativity are all rooted in Feminine experience. When cultures erased the Feminine, they stripped sanctity from women and erased devotion to the very forces that make life worth living.

Grief was framed as a weakness. Pleasure was condemned as a sin. Mystery was treated as a threat.

Stripped of the Feminine and stretched by the overreach of the Masculine, meaning is reduced to something earned or justified through productivity. When those fail to satisfy our need for true meaning, the soul collapses. That collapse is the vacuum we now inhabit.

This crisis runs through every layer of existence. It is more than politics, psychology, or economics. It is a crisis of disconnection.

We see it everywhere in epidemic levels of anxiety, depression, and burnout. Culture is built on numbing, rushing, producing, and escaping. We extract from the planet, from one another, and from ourselves. Relationships turn into performances. Nervous systems remain in a constant state of alert. We forget how to rest and how to truly feel.

This is not only psychological. It is spiritual displacement. We suffer from severing ourselves from Source and losing our place in the greater fabric of life.

Without the Feminine to balance it, the Masculine colonizes. Unmoored from its counterpart, Masculine energy grows rigid. Structure hardens into dogma. Action turns into aggression. Truth sharpens into weaponry. The Masculine, stripped of balance, becomes a tool for domination.

This is the world we inhabit, ruled by disembodiment, control, and abstraction. Without the Feminine, we cannot rest into our bodies. We lose the sacred rhythms of life that pulse through all of us. We cannot locate inner belonging, and we mistake survival for living.

You can feel it in your core.

Our Sacred Task

Beneath it all, something still remembers. The body remembers. The spirit remembers. Life is not earned. Life is lived, felt, and shared. In remembrance, we reclaim what was never anyone's to take.

This is not the end of the story.

You are not here to dismantle every system or destroy every institution. You are not called to wage war against the world you inherited. The task is to see clearly, to recognize distortion with calm clarity, to look without illusion and name, with truth, what has been broken in the name of progress.

You are here to reclaim your rhythm and balance. To reclaim your sovereignty. This doesn't begin with escape. It begins with awakening inside the very structures that once numbed, silenced, and shaped you.

The cultural systems that shape our lives don't need to stand as your enemy. They can stand as your mirror, reflecting both what has failed and what remains possible. They show the cost of forgetting and reveal the power of remembering, of turning inward, and of rising whole.

Every structure that fractured you, can open into a doorway. Every mechanism that controlled you can invite a restoration of what has always lived within you.

This is where the story begins anew. This is where you wake up.

When we awaken collectively, something extraordinary happens. The world realigns with the rhythm of Source. Systems shift through the way we choose to live from the inside out.

Through this act of alignment, we can reshape education, economy, medicine, and spirituality.

This is coherence in action. Disconnection breeds chaos. Imbalance breeds dysfunction. The systems built on domination and illusion are already collapsing under their own weight.

BEFORE WE FORGET

Sacred alignment is a return to the principles encoded within every one of us and throughout the natural world. When we step inward, we pave the way forward.

A society aligned with the Divine grows through collective integration. Progress is redefined through coherence and evolves from individual to collective truth.

This evolution reimagines education as wonder. Children are no longer taught to memorize and obey. They are encouraged to question, feel, and imagine. Wisdom matters more than performance. Learning becomes an act of liberation, not a preparation for obedience.

This evolution reshapes the economy around sufficiency. Worth is no longer measured by output. Wealth is no longer hoarded. Resources are shared instead of competed for. Time, care, and rest are once again held as sacred. Growth is no longer endless but cyclical and regenerative.

This evolution restores medicine as a union of body, mind, and spirit. The body is no longer seen as a malfunctioning machine but is honored as an intelligent vessel. Healing becomes holistic. Emotions are no longer pathologized. The nervous system and our stories all become part of the process. Wellness returns to its rightful place as a birthright, not a privilege.

And spirituality?

This evolution returns it to the people. It becomes unbranded and alive. It is no longer locked behind paywalls or polished into a product. We stop chasing awakening and begin embodying presence. We stop outsourcing divinity and begin remembering it.

We don't need to wage war on the system. We need to remember who we are within it. We begin with alignment, and from that alignment, we create something new.

The sacred lives within daily life, waiting to be remembered. The simple practices of attention, breath, rhythm, and feeling form the ground of individual and then societal transformation. Through these quiet openings, a sacred and eternal reclamation takes form.

Doorways

You do not need to escape the world to reclaim your soul. What was distorted can be clarified, and what was fragmented can be made whole. The Divine simply asks for participation.

The following doorways are pathways to return.

> **1. Trace Your Turning Point**
> Somewhere along the way, we traded presence for performance.
> Ask yourself gently:
> *When did I begin to doubt what I knew deep inside?*
> *Who taught me to seek permission to live with integrity?*
> *Where did I first abandon my rhythm?*
> Let these questions move through you. Do not rush the answers. Feel them. Witness where you first fractured, and let your awareness spark the return.
>
> **2. Use the Systems as Your Mirror**
> The next time you feel tension within a system, whether at work, in healthcare, school, or at home, pause.
> Ask yourself gently:
> *What is this moment reflecting back to me?*
> *What truth within me is asking to be remembered right now?*
> Instead of reacting, let the discomfort you feel become a teacher. Thank it. Then choose something more aligned.
>
> **3. Return to Your Presence**
> No performance. No ritual checklist. Just a moment of calm.
> Sit on the ground. Feel your breath. Place your hand on your heart or your belly.
> Ask yourself gently:
> *What part of me still remembers?*
> Listen without analyzing. Just feel yourself. Let this be your sacred space.

4. Reclaim One Ritual
Choose one ordinary act: eating, bathing, resting, or walking, and return it to your sacred rhythm. Slow down. Bring awareness to the texture, the breath, and the sensation.
Let your body become an altar. Let your attention be your prayer. When we infuse the mundane with devotion, the sacred reveals that it was never gone.

5. Treat Your Body as Your Temple
Your body is a sacred vessel that responds to rhythm.
Each day with coherent awareness touch something as a prayer, move as a ritual, and breathe as a sacred reminder that you are of the Divine.
Regulate your body to remind yourself that you are safe.
A calm nervous system is a portal back to Source.

6. Listen with Others
Offer your presence to someone without advice, analysis, or fixing. Just listen.
Hold space for them with patience, stillness, and care.
The sacred moves between us through attention.

Our Meditation

> Beneath the noise of our days
> moves a rhythm we did not invent.
> It runs through galaxies and oceans,
> through the seasons,
> through your heart.
>
> It stirred the first stars into being,
> and it still moves through you.
>
> The story of separation keeps us numb.
> It tells of a lifeless world,
> a distant God.

AARON SCOTT

It trains us to look upward instead of inward,
to seek permission instead of presence,
to confuse control with connection.

Centuries of forgetting bury the truth,
yet the field still moves through us.

The Divine is not an argument to win.
It is the pulse beneath every moment of life,
the knowing that arrives before thought,
the pull toward beauty we cannot explain.

The air you breathe has moved through forests.
Your bones carry minerals from ancient seas.
Your longing is the echo of home.
You were born from this connection.

Every choice you make,
every thought you feed,
shapes reality.
Creation does not happen around you.
It happens through you.

So pause.
Feel the hum beneath your skin.
Let it remind you.

You are part of Source.
You are one of its ways of seeing,
one of its ways of loving,
one of its ways of becoming.

Chapter 3
The Sleep Machine

The disconnection from the sacred that defines so much of modern life did not happen all at once. It unfolded gradually, as a series of shifts in worldview, each reinforcing the next. Over centuries, these shifts became embedded in institutions, ideologies, and collective behavior, forming the architecture of a society that normalizes disconnection as the foundation of reality.

Today, the mechanization of the body, the commodification of nature, and the fragmentation of knowledge feel ordinary. But they are not accidental. They are the result of a lineage, a deep pattern shaped by metaphysical, theological, and scientific assumptions that have been carried forward through religion, reason, and economy.

Severing Our Sanctity

In medieval Europe, the Catholic Church entrenched hierarchy and gave it spiritual authority. The cosmos was imagined as a vertical structure, with God above, man below, and nature beneath both. Divine access was mediated by clergy, scripture, and doctrine. The sacred was lifted out of the body, the Earth, and the immediate personal experience, and relocated to the heavens and the abstract.

The Church's hierarchical structure became the blueprint for how modern institutions have been organized and, maybe more importantly, how people relate to them. Framed as sacred and unchanging, it normalized authority flowing from the top down and obedience rising from the bottom up. Politics, education, medicine, media, and the economy later reproduced this same design. We see it when media outlets declare a narrative and it is treated as unquestionable truth, when health authorities issue directives that go unchallenged, and when clergy pronounce judgments that are received as final. In these cases, we rarely look deeper, question motives, or demand evidence, even when such declarations shape the most consequential choices of our lives.

By responding this way, we surrender agency to institutional intermediaries and outsource discernment and permission to those who claim sanctioned authority. Over time, this hierarchy became the operating system of modern power, sustained by our deference.

The Lie of the Matter

When Enlightenment thinkers like Descartes and Newton emerged, they did not dismantle the old hierarchical worldview; they secularized it. Spirit was replaced with science. Divine order became mechanical law. Descartes's dualism split mind from body and crowned rationality as the primary source of truth. Newton's cosmos operated like a clockwork machine, governed by fixed, predictable, and measurable laws.

In this new framework, mystery became a flaw and subjectivity a liability. Knowledge no longer required personal connection; it required distance, analysis, and control. Nature, once regarded as alive and intelligent, was reclassified as an inert resource to be studied, mastered, and used.

This was the birth of scientific materialism. This metaphysical stance asserts that reality consists only of what can be measured, that objective, observer-independent phenomena define the bounds of truth, and that consciousness, soul, and meaning are not fundamental but incidental byproducts.

This epistemology still underpins modern economic and political systems, where reality is often equated with whatever fits into a metric. Anything outside the ledger becomes secondary or invisible. Nowhere is this clearer than in the global reliance on Gross Domestic Product, or GDP, as the primary measure of societal progress. Despite decades of critique, GDP continues to dictate policy, reducing human flourishing to financial output while sidelining emotional well-being, spiritual depth, environmental health, and cultural integrity. In this paradigm, purpose, meaning, and consciousness are treated as irrelevant. This is the direct consequence of a worldview that defines truth by measurement and dismisses the immeasurable as unworthy of consideration.

Yet today, this worldview is buckling from the very sciences that once upheld it. Quantum physics dismantles the idea of a purely objective, observer-independent reality, revealing instead a participatory universe in which the observer is woven into the fabric of events. At the same time, neuroscience tells us that consciousness, intention, and self-awareness cannot be fully explained as mere products of brain chemistry. It appears that the mind does not emerge from matter but is fundamental to matter itself.

These revelations expose the limits of a mechanistic, reductionist worldview. And yet, we continue to organize our societies according to this outdated operating system. A system that mistakes its tools for truth and its measurements for reality itself.

Scaling Disconnection

Once the world had been desacralized and made measurable, it could be industrialized. The mechanistic worldview was embodied in factories, machines, and labor systems. Capitalism, socialism, and even state communism all drew from this same logic. Human value was defined by productivity; human beings and the Earth were both reduced to input, and time was reorganized around output.

Contemporary corporate and economic systems offer countless examples of how our society prioritizes and rewards linearity, efficiency, control, and unchecked growth. One of the most influential frameworks behind this mindset was articulated by economist Milton Friedman, whose doctrine of shareholder primacy became deeply embedded in U.S. corporate governance. According to this view, a company's only legitimate responsibility is to maximize profits for its shareholders, even when doing so undermines employee well-being, community health, or environmental sustainability. This ethos is reinforced by the economic mythology of "trickle-down" economics, which claims that concentrating wealth at the top will inevitably benefit all. In practice, it functions as a narrative shield for policies that place corporate and capital interests at the peak of the hierarchy, legitimizing wealth concentration while masking the reality that the promised benefits rarely reach those at the bottom. When corporations, money, and greed are left unchecked under the guise of necessary economic expansion or job creation, corruption becomes inevitable, and every other value, from ecological care to human dignity, is pushed into secondary importance.

In this arrangement, the human being becomes a commodity, valued only for their capacity to generate profit, regardless of the cost. Life is reduced to output, productivity, and efficiency, while well-being, purpose, and connection are dismissed as irrelevant. This is not simply the illusion of separation magnified; it is a profound betrayal of the Divine itself.

Internalizing Systems

Today, our institutions continue to carry these embedded logics. Our schools mirror factories. Our hospitals treat bodies as malfunctioning systems. Our governments serve power, not people.

The most insidious outcome is that these systems hide their construction and present themselves as inevitable. They design our separation from nature, from one another, and from the sacred. Over time, we internalize that design.

While the machine may operate outside of us, it programs our inner world.

From early childhood, we are trained to perform, to produce, and to please. We learn to hide our emotions, carrying them like shameful weight. We learn to push aside our wonder, treating curiosity as if it were a distraction. We learn to doubt the fire of our own originality, fearing it will set us apart. Even when we rest, we turn against ourselves, believing that pausing makes us weak.

By adulthood, these lessons no longer come from outside. They live inside us. We manage ourselves like machines, measuring our worth by what we produce. We chase belonging by molding ourselves to fit the very norms that fracture our souls.

Deep down, you know it. You feel it.

Generational trauma lives on in us, shaping patterns we rarely notice. Our families, our religions, and our institutions pass down scarcity and shame as though they were common sense. What begins as survival becomes inheritance, etched into the fabric of each new generation. Even our rebellions, meant to free us, often repeat the same pattern. We resist control with control instead of remembering how to live in coherence.

Now the machine has gone digital. Its logic of efficiency and extraction spreads through the rhythms of daily life. We trade presence for screens. We let notifications splinter our stillness. We curate ourselves for performance on social media. In the end, stimulation floods every corner of our lives and silence becomes a stranger.

As a civilization we have more content than ever before, yet we are starving for meaning. Information multiplies at a rate we cannot absorb, while wisdom slips further from reach. Our nervous systems remain braced in survival as we drown in input. As a result our disconnection deepens as the sacred recedes into memory.

Perhaps the greatest loss is our living cosmology. Our ancestors saw the world alive. The forest was their family, and the stars were their teachers. Ritual, myth, and story placed them in relationship with the whole of existence. We have traded that way of seeing for abstraction. We have reduced myth to marketing and outsource our meaning to systems that cannot feel.

Our soul waits patiently for us to remember.

Quiet Remembering

Before we remember, we must understand what we've been shaped to forget.

The mechanistic worldview shaped more than machines. It shaped people to act like machines. Generations were trained to obey, to optimize, and to measure their worth by how efficiently they could function within systems that denied their souls. The human spirit, once central to life, was pushed to the margins. The institutions we sanctified didn't honor the sacred; they sought to control it.

The legacy of this paradigm runs through our time. We see it in pharmaceutical industries that suppress symptoms instead of healing root causes. We see it in schools that reduce intelligence to tests and categories. We see it in governments that build bureaucracies designed for control rather than care. We see it in economies that extract relentlessly and call it progress.

This is the tragedy we live with. These systems dominate our lives, and they are built on a delusional reality. The universe is alive. Life is irreducible. Human beings are not hardware waiting to be optimized. The mechanistic lens may be useful for invention and productivity, but it was never meant to serve as our ideology.

To reclaim our lives, we must recognize that these systems grew out of a civilization that forgot its relational intelligence. We forgot the sacredness of emotion and the living intelligence of the Earth itself. The reality we occupy today is not one built on coherence but anchored in fragmentation.

And yet we remember.

If distortion can be designed and absorbed, then so can its antidote. Now that we see how the machine was built, we can begin to imagine how to dismantle it.

We power it down with truth. One soul at a time.

Glorified Sleep

We live in a world that has forgotten its sacred roots, so it is no surprise that capitalism has been glorified. This wasn't done consciously. Most were shaped by it long before they had the chance to question it. We inhabit a society that drifts in a kind of sleep. Not careless, not unintelligent, but caught in a trance. A dream carried through generations. A dream of progress, success, growth, and self-worth measured only in external terms.

This is not a condemnation of the capitalist model. It is a recognition of our blind acceptance of it.

To understand how capitalism came to occupy the center of the modern imagination, we have to look at the soil where it took root. It emerged in a world already stripped of its enchantment, where nature had lost its spirit, the body its wisdom, and the soul its voice. The sacred was pushed into the sky, and the sacred Feminine was subdued. Human life was reorganized around extraction, output, and control. Capitalism did not invent fragmentation, but it flourished within it. It built its logic on hierarchy, extraction, separation, and dominance.

Over time, capitalism began to offer what felt like purpose. It replaced the mystery of life with structure, supplanted presence with identity, and filled in meaning with reward. It promised progress, and it delivered visible results such as wealth, innovation, and industrial expansion. For a society already disconnected from inner worth and collective belonging, capitalism appeared to be the answer. It became more than an economic model. It became a belief system.

And so, it was glorified.

This took hold because capitalism mirrored the deeper logic of a society that had learned to trust only what could be seen, counted, owned, or sold. It fit the mechanized world like a glove. It offered people a sense of control in an uncertain universe, and it gave them a ladder when they had forgotten their roots.

This glorification is not unique to capitalism. Alternatives such as socialism have also struggled under the same spiritual weight. Socialism often arises in response to the imbalances of capitalism, lifting up ideals of equality, shared resources, and justice. Yet its fate depends on the consciousness that holds it. Under corrupt leadership, socialism has often consolidated power more tightly than capitalism, suppressing dissent through mandates and replacing economic inequality with ideological control.

History shows us that socialist experiments, though born from equity, reproduce the same patterns of centralization and disconnection when they are rooted in fragmentation. This is not an attack on socialism itself. It is a reminder that any system severed from the sacred and from relational wisdom will eventually mirror the very dynamics it sought to resist.

Whether capitalist or socialist, corporate or state-controlled, when the guiding consciousness is greed, domination, fear, or hollow efficiency, the outcomes look alike. We see control spreading. We see dissent silenced. We see life commodified. We see humanity reduced to function, only under different names. When Masculine logic, structure, and order are not balanced with Feminine compassion, intuition, and relationship, systems turn rigid. When power is cut off from wisdom, corruption follows. When survival replaces the soul, every model eventually collapses inward.

This is not a call to demonize capitalism, nor to dismiss the ideals of socialism. There are no villains in a story of forgetting. Systems are tools, and tools reflect the consciousness of those who hold them.

To glorify any model without questioning the mind and heart that sustain it is to mistake the map for the journey. The issue is not one of ideology but of the absence of coherence. It is a collective amnesia that blinds us to what a sacred, interconnected world could look like.

To awaken from this spell does not mean rejecting everything that has been built. It means seeing clearly, recognizing what no longer serves, and restoring what was lost.

There can be a time when systems serve life instead of life serving systems. When economics bows to ecology, and when worth is measured by all the necessary and fundamental aspects of our whole lived reality.

To reimagine and rebuild our world, we must look more closely at how mechanized systems have trained us to think, to feel, and to belong.

Education

What we call education is often the first place children are introduced to sedation. Here, the sacred pulse of wonder is measured, timed, and weighed. Children arrive with instinctive wisdom, eager to explore, but instead of being guided to deepen that inner compass, they are taught to override it.

Their obedience is rewarded, and their curiosity, unless it fits within pre-approved boundaries, is redirected or punished. Children learn quickly that it is safer to follow instructions than to question. They instinctively sense that it is safer to repeat than to explore. As with all of these systems, the external replaces the internal as the primary source of truth. Grades and standardized scores become education's currency of value.

This model did not arise by accident. It mirrors the industrial logic it was designed to serve. In early twentieth-century America, John D. Rockefeller helped institutionalize an education system that prioritized obedience. Through the General Education Board, he directed vast funding into public schooling, reshaping it in the image of factory production.

Rockefeller's advisor, Frederick T. Gates, once wrote, "In our dream, we have limitless resources, and the people yield themselves with perfect docility to our molding hand." Their goal was to create a compliant and predictable workforce.

As early as 1914, the National Education Association voiced concern that philanthropic foundations, including Rockefeller's and Carnegie's, were exerting influence over educational policy in ways that undermined democratic freedom. Even after World War II, congressional oversight exposed how several tax-exempt foundations had coordinated efforts to steer public education toward a controlled and utilitarian agenda.

Education was once a way of aligning with the inner self, but it has been reshaped into a system for managing human minds. The dreamer, the artist, and the critical thinker are recast as problems to solve. This system has boxed thoughts into compartments while treating feelings as interference. The body has been stripped of meaning and is valued only as a vessel for competition on the field. The regimented schedule of school silences the natural rhythm of the child, and the many voices of external authority begin to replace the quiet guidance of the child's inner teacher.

Students have learned to live primarily in their heads, cut off from their bodies, their feelings, and their intuition. Knowledge becomes something to consume, and as the child's imagination fades, their expressions narrow. In the end, the curiosity and untamed wonder that belong to childhood are trained out, little by little.

The fracture is subtle but profound. A child whose inner knowing is dismissed again and again begins to doubt it was ever real. They turn outward for answers and learn to live from the outside in. As that fracture deepens, it becomes harder to reclaim their voice, their rhythm, and eventually their soul.

This is more than a problem of schooling. It reaches into the spiritual heart of our lives. When we sedate our children, we sever the thread that ties them to the sacred within.

Media

If education trains the mind to perform, media trains the nervous system to react. In a world shaped by attention economies, the media acts as both a mirror of culture and one of its most powerful engineers. What it engineers is reactivity.

Movie studios, streaming platforms, and social media companies employ neuroscientists, behavioral psychologists, and data analysts to design content that activates our most primal responses. Fear, outrage, and sexual stimulation bypass rational thought, hooking directly into the limbic system. The amygdala lights up, the nervous system jolts into alertness, and higher reasoning takes a back seat. In this state, content is internalized without any real discernment.

Production companies score soundtracks to induce adrenaline and dopamine rushes. Edits are timed to mimic neural entrainment patterns, and narratives are optimized to trigger the strongest emotional reactions. Conflict, ridicule, and seduction are the currencies of attention, and attention, in this architecture, is a commodity to be bought, sold, and mined.

This is not to say that all media is manipulative or all storytelling is harmful, but the dominant media landscape is shaped by incentives that do not serve awakening. It thrives on reaction and repetition and rewards polarization over nuance. And yet, with all of this stimulation, no one is satisfied.

In this environment, awakening becomes an act of resistance. It means reclaiming your attention as a sacred resource. It means noticing how your body feels when you scroll, binge, or absorb someone else's projection of reality. It means choosing to engage consciously.

When you track your reactivity, you begin to disrupt the cycle. You start to notice what pulls you out of yourself and what helps you return. You observe rather than absorb, and in that moment, you are no longer just a consumer. You are a sovereign participant.

You can still enjoy a film, story, or feed, but now you do it awake. You see the framing, the hooks, the cues, and more importantly, you see yourself. You become aware of your triggers, desires, and patterns. The screen becomes a mirror, and looking into it with awareness is a sacred act. We shift from sleep into presence.

At its best, media is a portal to beauty, connection, and expanded perception. Yet in its current architecture, it often functions as anesthesia. This isn't about abandoning media, but about reentering it consciously and engaging with discernment.

What you give your attention to, you give your life to. When you remember that, you become unprogrammable.

Medicine

The modern medical industry emerged from a worldview that imagined the body as a machine and its symptoms as faults to be corrected. In the process, it stripped away the understanding that healing is rooted in the sacred bond between the Earth, the soul, and the community. Stories were recast to portray the old ways as dangerous and unsanitary, though they carried far more truth and wisdom than we were led to believe.

As industry gathered force, medicine hardened into a mechanistic form. The body was treated as an object to be managed, illness was stripped of its story, and the voices of fatigue and grief fell silent. What had once been an art of restoration narrowed into the task of regulation and symptom suppression.

This transformation bore the imprint of money and power. In 1910, the Flexner Report, backed by Carnegie and Rockefeller foundations, reshaped medical education across the United States and Canada. Schools that held herbal, homeopathic, and indigenous traditions were extinguished, while women healers, already persecuted for centuries, were erased under the banner of progress. What remained was a single paradigm that trained doctors to diagnose with machines and to treat patients primarily with drugs. It's no coincidence that illness is rarely treated with natural remedies, since pharmaceutical companies cannot patent them or profit from their sale. We have been led to believe this is acceptable, but we rarely ask, "Acceptable for whose benefit?"

Chemical intervention soon took center stage, with institutions defining legitimacy while pharmaceutical industries expanded in parallel, financing the very systems that upheld their authority. The deeper purpose of medicine, to restore harmony, to listen to the body, and to heal with care, was buried beneath the weight of protocols, insurance codes, and productivity metrics. In this design, the doctor stood as the authority, the patient was reduced to a file, and the body became a collection of components to be optimized. Chronic illness was medicated rather than understood, and the central question shifted from what the body was saying to how quickly it could be returned to function. Care narrowed into treatment.

Yet symptoms carry meaning. They speak the language of memory, trauma, lineage, and unmet need. When muted, their messages dissolve into silence, and the body's wisdom is lost.

The brilliance of modern medicine shines most brightly in moments of crisis, when a bone shatters in an accident, when a heart falters without warning, or when an infection that once meant certain death is met with astonishing skill. In these moments we glimpse the beauty of human ingenuity.

Beyond the emergency room, another story unfolds. Chronic illness spreads quietly, fed by stress and loneliness, by toxic food and poisoned environments, and it catches full blaze in the relentless pace of modern life.

Health itself has become an enormous industry. Pharmaceutical corporations design models that reward endless treatment and lifelong prescriptions more than prevention, until the logic of the marketplace eclipses the sacred logic of life. The measure of medicine shifts from whether it heals to whether it sells.

Here lies the fracture at the heart of our culture. We are kept alive but rarely kept whole, and to recover our health, we must remember how medicine is meant to serve us, not the other way around.

The structure of our systems reveals a stark paradox. The same machinery that fills our food with artificial flavors, pesticides, and metals also provides the drugs to treat the illnesses born of those substances. Autoimmune disorders, hormonal collapse, and cancers rising quietly in the body reflect an economy that prizes profit above human life itself, weaving illness and treatment into the same design. Organic and non-GMO foods, once treated as luxuries, now stand as necessities.

The loop refines itself with precision. Chemicals are praised as innovation, food is engineered for taste without nourishment, bodies weaken, and pharmaceuticals arrive at the doctor's office or hospital to manage the decline. Cause and cure circulate together, completing the circuit of a beautifully well-oiled machine.

Our awakening to the state of our health crises begins with awareness. To notice what we put into our bodies, and to choose what sustains rather than what sedates or stimulates, is to step out of the cycle of profit and hypnosis and return to living awake with dignity.

Economy

The modern economy is more than a method of exchange. It has become a faith, a belief system whose central prayer is simple and unyielding. You are what you produce.

From the earliest days of childhood, we are taught to measure our worth in output. We are taught that to be valuable is to be useful and that to be good is to be productive. Rest carries the sting of weakness. Even care, that most natural of human instincts, is dismissed if it cannot be monetized or accounted for on a ledger.

This creed is both cultural and structural. Our systems are built to keep people in survival mode, chasing accumulation that never quite arrives. Enough is never enough. The goalpost always moves, pulling us deeper into a rhythm of consumption, competition, and conquest that is etched into the very fabric of the marketplace.

Busyness becomes a badge of honor and hustle a moral imperative. The tired worker is praised while the well-rested one is questioned. It's no revelation to say that our calendars are full and our spirits are starving. We treat our bodies as tools and scrutinize our hours as though commodities. What truly nourishes life, such as tending to children, bonding with the elderly, even caring for our communities, is erased from the economy's ledgers. These acts create no profit, so they are rendered invisible.

This is no failure. It is the perfection of overextended capitalism. A machine that rewards effort while extracting it and that praises growth without asking what is being grown. In this system we idolize wealth without counting the cost of its accumulation. In the end, all of our time collapses into tasks and our presence is sacrificed at the altar of productivity.

People burn out because they are caught in a structure that extracts endlessly and replenishes rarely. The extraction is celebrated, dressed up as ambition, drive, and success. Yet within, we feel socially disconnected, internally fragmented, and eternally exhausted. We manage life as though it were an industrial project rather than living it as the mystery it was meant to be. The most entranced explain it away as normal life, yet beneath the illusion lies nothing but externally imposed madness.

This model does not end with us. It is passed down like inheritance. Parents, in pursuit of security, guide their children into the very institutions that shaped them. Schools rehearse the values of the marketplace, teaching performance, obedience, and comparison. Children learn quickly that approval is not given for being but for achieving. Long before the soul learns to rest, it learns to hustle.

And still, fragments of truth continue to slip through. Our grandparents remind us that life is too short and that money cannot buy happiness. These are not cliches. They are the distilled truths of wise elders who have already been there and done that. At the end of the chase, we discover our longing for connection, meaning, and sufficiency was never in the chase at all.

Government

In its sacred origin, governance was meant to embody care. It was a relational structure designed to uphold reciprocity between people, land, and the greater whole. In its highest form, governance protected the commons, amplified collective wisdom, and preserved balance across generations.

But in the modern world, governance has drifted from this sacred origin. It has become a machinery of power, often more concerned with preserving institutional continuity than serving collective well-being. Its decisions are made at a distance through metrics that direct policies written to protect systems, not people. In our present framework, power has become its own feedback loop, insulated from the very people it was meant to represent.

This transformation did not occur in a single era or by the will of a single group. It unfolded through decades of economic consolidation, political lobbying, bureaucratic expansion, and the steady prioritization of institutional survival over our collective care.

In the United States, these dynamics became increasingly visible throughout the twentieth century. Regulatory agencies such as the Food and Drug Administration and the Environmental Protection Agency were created to serve the public interest. Yet both have frequently been shaped by what legal scholars call "regulatory capture," where the industries meant to be regulated exert influence through lobbying, personnel appointments, and long-term funding relationships. Former executives of pharmaceutical, agricultural, and chemical corporations are often appointed to leadership roles within these agencies and later return to private-sector positions. This revolving door creates a conflict of interest so blatant it should shatter public trust, yet it persists in plain sight.

Similarly, philanthropic foundations have wielded profound influence over public discourse. The Reece Committee of 1953, a congressional investigation, examined the extent to which tax-exempt foundations, such as those of Rockefeller, Carnegie, and Ford, had come to shape policy, research, and academia. Though the investigation was cut short and remains controversial, it raised important questions about how unelected, well-funded institutions can steer national direction behind the scenes. This influence, in a remarkable fashion, typically occurs without transparency or democratic accountability.

We also see bipartisan consensus around policies that protect elite financial interests while offering little systemic relief to the public. After the 2008 financial collapse, both major political parties supported a $700 billion bailout for Wall Street institutions. Meanwhile, millions of citizens lost homes, jobs, and retirement savings. Similarly, defense spending has expanded consistently under both Republican and Democratic leadership, while domestic infrastructure, education, and healthcare remain chronically underfunded. This is no oversight.

The appearance of conflict in mainstream politics often masks deep alignment when it comes to preserving economic and geopolitical dominance. While social issues dominate public debate, major legislative decisions on war, trade, surveillance, and corporate regulation are consistently passed with bipartisan support. Rhetoric on "freedom," "economic growth," or "security" is recycled across party lines, yet it rarely corresponds to meaningful transformation.

This is, yet again, the predictable result of systems optimized for continuity and self-interest.

When governance forgets its sacred purpose, it becomes a mechanism of self-preservation. It no longer exists to serve but rather to sustain itself. Its legitimacy becomes performative, and its priorities become shaped less by collective need and more by proximity to influence.

Yet the sacred potential remains.

True governance begins with care and coherence. It values transparency, accountability, and truth as core design principles.

We cannot rely solely on top-down reform, but we can begin to restore sacred governance from the bottom up. In our communities, organizations, and personal spheres of influence, we can model leadership that is relational, participatory, and rooted in connection.

We resurrect sacred governance by realigning it with integrity.

The Human Consequence

In the modern world, sleep no longer waits for darkness. It is crafted in plain sight and woven into systems that quiet our senses and tame the sacred connections that once kept us awake to life. This architecture of sedation secures obedience through habits we repeat until they feel natural, and through the subtle penalties that follow curiosity.

This sleep pulls us away from our inner life, severing our connection to the body's intelligence and to the rhythms of the world that move around us. It carries us through the motions of living without ever allowing us to inhabit life fully. Over time, it becomes an unconscious trance, woven so deeply into culture that repetition makes it appear as nothing more than normal life.

We notice it in the smallest moments, and if we are honest, we feel it in ourselves. Our hand reaches for the phone before our first breath has even settled in the lungs. Our voices move through conversations while our attention drifts elsewhere, never fully hearing or being heard. We slip into the cycles of working, consuming, responding, and producing, and we forget to ask why. In those moments, we treat the body like a machine and forget that it is a living ecosystem, full of awareness, that never stops speaking. We forget that every choice shapes the soul, not just the schedule.

The systems that hold us in this sleep hum inside our lives, soft but steady, until we begin to mistake their rhythm for our own. We start believing that performance is who we are, that rest is weakness, and that meaning is something we must prove.

And yet the sacred refuses to be silenced, for even when we are lost in the trance, something in us stays awake. We feel it when calmness arrives and unsettles us with its strangeness. We feel it in a breath that settles deeper than the pull of distraction. We feel it in the ache that rises in the chest or belly, whispering, *This is not it.* We may not know exactly what is being remembered, but we feel the absence of the Divine that once held us whole. Our bodies strain under the weight of disconnection, and our minds, though crowded, hunger for life.

Remembering begins here, in sensation. It begins when our nervous system softens for a moment or our breath slows and deepens. Our presence returns without effort, opening a threshold we did not plan. It becomes an invitation back to ourselves.

The machinery of sleep feeds on our unconsciousness. It grows stronger each time we abandon ourselves, each time we silence our instincts, each time we treat our bodies as tools. But the moment we pause, the moment we draw a full breath and feel it, the spell weakens and the trance begins to break.

Awakening simply asks us to see clearly. It asks that we notice and name what has been taken, and that we recognize the system is not who we are. It is a conditioning laid over us.

The machinery was never the truth, and it will never set you free.

The Sleeping Toll

When our systems prize productivity over meaning, the cost is a slow collective cultural sedation.

BEFORE WE FORGET

When we live in constant reaction, pulled by habit and pressed into continuous motion, we skim across the surface of life and lose touch with its depth. Our nervous systems adapt by numbing, our feelings blur into one another until grief feels like fatigue, our anger tightens into anxiety, and our joy overwhelms like overstimulation. What was once our compass begins to feel like a burden to manage or suppress. This is how we survive, but the cost is steep. Over time, we lose the intelligence of our emotions and the capacity to feel fully. We allow those manipulated feelings to guide us.

In a culture that never stops moving, we forget how to rest. Burnout seeps in until it feels normal. Together we become overextended and undernourished. The collective body is weary because the systems we live inside demand that we override ourselves at every turn. And since success is measured by productivity, our exhaustion is treated as a personal flaw rather than the signal of a culture in collapse.

The deepest cost of this unrelenting pace is spiritual amnesia. We forget who we are, what we carry, and where we belong. The sacred does not vanish, but it grows harder to feel. Intuition quiets. Wonder dims, and deep connection becomes rare. This has nothing to do with religion or belief and has everything to do with healthy relationships. When our relationships with every aspect of life decay, the meaning of life itself slips through our fingers.

We may not be empty, but we are estranged, and this estrangement opens into a quiet crisis of orientation. We all sense that something is wrong, but we struggle to name it for what it is.

Estrangement, however, is not the end of our story. When we allow ourselves to arrive fully, and to rest gently into the present, we begin to awaken our sacred essence that has always been there.

The Divine has not condemned us; it has only been waiting for us to return.

Distorted Identity and Values

The machinery of sleep does more than sedate behavior. It distorts our identity and rewires the very way we see ourselves, others, and the world around us. It shifts our internal compass from essence to appearance and performance. In this world, identity is molded by systems that reward our output, visibility, and alignment with external norms.

We treat ourselves as commodities. We measure our worth by how much we produce, how others perceive us, and how well we fit the script. We push our souls aside and call it fantasy. We even turn our backs on ourselves by dismissing our intuition as irrational and deeming our search for greater depth inconvenient.

So, we adapt, often unconsciously. We edit ourselves, market ourselves, and tailor our lives to meet the demands of algorithms, institutions, employers, and social consensus. We begin to believe we are only as worthy as we are useful and only as lovable as we are attractive or productive. In the end, our value is outsourced to external validation.

This performance becomes exhausting. It scrapes away our authenticity and we end up curating ourselves instead of honoring our own individual truth. And with every layer of curation, we lose the richness that makes life meaningful.

The loss doesn't stop with the individual self. If I don't know who I truly am, how can I truly see you? Our interactions become transactional, and we assess people by status, usefulness, or similarity. We habitually compare more than connect, and tend to judge instead of listen. Our vulnerability begins to feel unsafe, and our emotional truth becomes a liability. So we mask and perform for the machine.

As a result, our values become distorted. We begin to worship only what is visible, monetizable, and measurable. Money, image, influence, and control become the gods we serve. Our very own ethics bend under the weight of our ambition, and our integrity becomes optional in this culture obsessed with achievement.

This is precisely how fragmentation becomes normalized. But this is not our human nature. It is our cultural conditioning, and it is the direct result of inhabiting systems that confuse function with fulfillment. We are not broken. We are being pulled away from our sacred selves.

To reclaim our identity is to remember that we are not the sum of our achievements. We are our awareness and our spirit. We are a sacred connection. We have never been a competition.

If we are to restore our values, we must return care to the center of our lives. We must measure success by how aligned we are internally, by how present we are with those we love, and by how honestly we express what is true.

Artificial Intelligence

Artificial intelligence is the logical extension of a worldview that treats consciousness as computation, life as data, and intelligence as pattern recognition divorced from soul. It emerges from the same mechanistic cosmology that once reduced the body to machinery, nature to dead matter, and the cosmos to a lifeless system of law. AI development, in its current framework, unconsciously accelerates this worldview.

The architects of artificial intelligence are not spiritual elders or ecological trustees. They are venture capitalists, defense contractors, data miners, and global tech giants. Major technology companies and their affiliates collaborate with powerful governmental and military institutions to train machines that imitate human cognition. The goal has never been to deepen our humanity but rather to replicate and surpass it through simulation.

This project is framed as progress, even destiny. Proponents of the "Singularity" suggest that merging with machines is humanity's next step. There are many executives in the technology sector who envision a future where consciousness is uploaded and mortality is overcome. Even some that promote the idea that we must integrate with AI to survive. In both cases, the human body is seen as obsolete hardware, the soul becomes irrelevant, and consciousness is redefined as computation. These visions are born from a paradigm that equates evolution with enhancement and intelligence with domination.

But this is not evolution. It is inversion. It is a simulated mirror of spiritual growth that reflects our confusion rather than our coherence. In this mirror, efficiency and imitation replace wisdom.

The belief that we can build sentient machines presumes that we understand sentience. The truth is that we have not resolved the nature of our own awareness, so how can we engineer what we do not yet comprehend? To recreate intelligence without acknowledging its emotional, intuitive, and sacred dimensions is not progress, it is projection. It is the extension of a fragmented self into code.

And who benefits from this projection? The same institutions that have long profited from control. Corporations seek to automate labor and monetize attention. Governments pursue predictive surveillance. Military contractors develop autonomous weapons. Financial institutions deploy algorithmic trading systems that respond faster than any human ever could. These are not accidental outcomes. They are built into the structure. In this system, intelligence is stripped of soul and programmed for profit.

What we call artificial intelligence is not truly intelligent. It is trained on massive datasets scraped from human output. It mimics language but cannot feel. It reflects patterns but cannot intuit. It can replicate expression but not originate meaning. Despite this, we are asked to replace the human with the machine in therapy, medicine, customer service, and even education. We are asked yet again to replace the living with what is artificial.

This is an acute crisis of meaning.

AI is being heralded as the next leap in evolution, but in truth, it reveals how far we have drifted from our essence. We have not remembered the sacred intelligence that breathes through life. We have not yet healed the rupture between mind and body, or intellect and intuition. To build machines in our image while still estranged from our inner alignment is to scale confusion, not consciousness.

If we do not understand our own sacred intelligence, how can we possibly engineer its successor? Until we remember that intelligence is not merely the capacity to know but the capacity to care, connect, and create in alignment with life, we will not be building the future; we will only be replicating the distortion.

AI does not have to be the enemy, but it must not become our god.

To develop truly conscious technology would require a completely different foundation, one rooted in respect, interdependence, and humility. It would require asking both what is possible and what is wise. And it would demand restoring the sacred at the center of our design.

Until then, AI remains a mirror that doesn't reflect our evolution, but the apex of our disembodiment.

Cracks in the Machinery

When we begin to see through the machinery of sleep, what once seemed permanent begins to fracture. The spell doesn't break all at once, but in brief moments of clarity that remind us the world we inherited is not the world we must live in. The systems that trained us to override our body, distrust our emotions, and worship performance begins to tremble under the weight of its own incoherence.

The cracks appear first as discomfort. A gnawing sense that something essential is missing. An inability to keep up with expectations that never seem to end. A quiet grief that rises in stillness. We try to numb the feeling, outrun it, outwork it, but eventually, the fracture becomes visible. The system is not sustainable. The reward never satisfies. The chase never ends.

These moments are the places where the soul begins to push against the confines of the machine, and where the body refuses to keep performing for systems it does not trust. It's in these moments that the spirit whispers, *Enough.*

Through these cracks, we begin to see that our exhaustion was never personal and that our anxiety is not individual pathology. We see clearly that these are the byproducts of systemic design and the natural responses to a disembodied world. In these small ruptures, we realize that what we once carried as fault is, in truth, the first stirring of our awakening.

The cracks in the machinery are appearing all around us, visible in the disillusionment of workers who no longer recognize themselves in the jobs they perform, in teachers who ache to offer truth instead of tests, in doctors who entered medicine to heal yet find themselves confined to pharmaceutical company overlords, and in parents who feel in their bones that sending their children into another day of sedation is no longer something they can accept. These are signals of a deeper awakening moving through us as a collective.

What breaks through the cracks is never chaos. It is our clarity. It is a vision that reshapes the questions we carry. We begin to wonder what we truly believe in, who we are when stripped of production, what rhythms feel honest to our bodies, and what kind of life we wish to return to when we wake up each day. These are sacred invitations that guide us toward a reorientation of soul and society.

These cracks reveal that the old structures can no longer contain what is real. The sacred grows beyond the synthetic with coherence, until the shell gives way to something larger and more alive.

To break the spell, we withdraw our consent to let these systems define us. We remember the pulse of rest, the texture of feeling, and maybe most importantly, the power of conscious choosing. We stop rehearsing the roles we were given and start inhabiting the fullness of who we are. The task is to reclaim our worth from the grip of the world machinery.

The noise of these systems is relentless, yet beneath it the truth waits in stillness. It waits for us to slow down and listen.

This was never the fall of civilization and has always been the fall of illusion. And what rises through the cracks is simply our remembrance.

The Real Revolution

When one person returns to alignment, and lives from the rhythm of their own inner compass, they do more than heal themselves. They generate coherence, and coherence is contagious. As people begin to live in resonance with the sacred field, choosing work, time, and connection from a place of balance rather than survival, they emit a frequency that begins to inform the collective.

Models don't shift through mass compliance or performative rebellion. They evolve through energetic re-patterning that bleeds into the architecture of culture itself. Our evolution then becomes our revolution, and it is exactly why "the revolution will not be televised." The real revolution doesn't announce itself in headlines. It happens in nervous systems, in breath, in invisible refusals to rearrange ourselves to fit into the machine manual's specifications.

True revolution begins with conscious living and non-conformity. External systems, policies, and laws reflect the consciousness that created them, so to change them without first changing the underlying consciousness is to rearrange the theater seats while the play remains the same.

And yet, history has shown us what happens when this inner revolution is bypassed. When we attempt to restructure society without first restructuring the consciousness that animates it, we do not build something new; we replicate the very fractures we sought to escape, dressed in different languages and symbols. Time and again, human beings have mistaken external change through revolt for actual transformation. We have torn down monarchies, rewritten constitutions, toppled regimes, and rebranded ideologies, all while leaving untouched the deeper architecture of fear, separation, and control that shaped them.

Nowhere is this more evident than in the major revolutions of modern history, each of which promised liberation but, without the integration of sacred rhythm, yielded only reorganization. To understand why our systems continue to circle the same dysfunction, we must revisit these revolutions to reimagine what could have been possible if they had emerged from coherence.

The French Revolution is often celebrated as the dawn of modern democracy, an uprising against monarchy, religious control, and class oppression. However, although it succeeded in collapsing the aristocracy, it quickly descended into bloodshed, paranoia, and power struggles. The guillotine replaced the crown, and what was born was terror under a new regime.

Why? Because it addressed the structure, not the soul. The revolution's consciousness was born of trauma and reaction and was conditioned by vengeance. Revolution became a mass rupture and not a careful reintegration. And while it may not have explicitly targeted the sacred, it inherited a worldview already shaped by Enlightenment rationalism, which had long since privatized or dismissed the Divine as irrelevant to public life. The result was a revolution that sought justice without sanctity and reason devoid of rhythm.

In Russia, the 1917 revolution promised freedom from the feudal tsarist regime and a society built on equality. But in practice, it gave rise to an even more dehumanizing system of centralized control. Spirituality was outlawed, intuition was policed, and individual sovereignty was sacrificed in the name of collective productivity. This was a deliberate purge. The sacred was seen as a threat to uniformity and obedience. Monasteries were shuttered, mystics were persecuted, and a culture rich in ancestral depth was reduced to bureaucratic machinery.

This was a revolution devoid of inner coherence. Russian cultural DNA is characterized by deep mysticism, endurance, and a poetic connection to suffering and the land. Had these qualities been integrated into the revolution's foundation, a different form of social transformation could have emerged. Conscious leaders could have guided moral discourse. The Russian soul, when honored rather than suppressed, offers profound spiritual resilience, not authoritarianism.

The Chinese Communist Revolution sought to purge corruption and foreign domination, and return power to the people, but it did so by erasing the very essence of Chinese identity, ancestral wisdom, Taoist balance, Confucian order, and natural cosmology. During the Cultural Revolution, sacred texts were burned, elders were humiliated, and traditions were abolished. This was a surgical removal. The Divine was actively criminalized because the sacred threatens hierarchical power structures. In its place, China was thrown into industrial conformity. The system changed, but the collective psyche was driven deeper into fragmentation.

Across these revolutions, the failure was of comprehension. In each case, the sacred was absent, unconsciously omitted by Enlightenment frameworks in France and deliberately suppressed in Russia and China. Whether through inherited beliefs or overt enforcement, the Divine was excluded from the design. They sought external upheaval but required internal societal transformation. They replaced kings and empires but left untouched the root structure of separation, fear, and domination. Without reordering consciousness, no revolution can succeed because systems simply reassemble into new versions of the same "dis-ease."

But if these revolutions, and many others, had begun with the sacred; if they had emerged from the collective aching need for rhythm, inner freedom, and embodied belonging, the worlds that followed would have looked entirely different. None of these imagined societies would have been perfect, but they would have been coherent.

Sacred rhythm is the underlying intelligence of all living systems. When a society mirrors the cosmic flow, stays in tune with sacred rhythm, and values integration, it becomes inherently sustainable.

This is the architecture of all resilient ecosystems. It is biology, physics, and truth. It is civilization remembering how to live in resonance with, not in opposition to, life itself.

Our Meditation

> This chapter is not about despair.
> It is about decoding the system.

AARON SCOTT

It's easy to feel overwhelmed
when we glimpse the architecture of fragmentation,
woven into our schools,
into our medicine,
into our economy,
into the patterns of daily life.

But clarity is a gift.
Awareness is the beginning of sovereignty.

To awaken is to step outside the machinery,
to stop being carried by its rhythm.
To stop confusing performance with presence,
productivity with purpose,
numbness with peace.

The system may continue to turn,
but it no longer turns through you.
The soul has not been lost.
It has only been lulled into sleep.
Beneath the habits of disconnection,
beneath the weight of survival and expectation,
something remains untouched,
unbroken,
whole.

You do not need to dismantle the world
to find your place within it.
You need only begin here,
with your body,
with your breath,
with the truth you still carry.

BEFORE WE FORGET

The machine,
with all its systems and strategies,
has a fatal design flaw.
It runs on participation.

It needs our belief.
Our energy.
Our agreement.

That means we have more power than we think.

The moment we stop unconsciously playing along,
we begin to rewrite the script.

So, what does that look like?

It begins with noticing.
Pay attention to what drains your life force.

Where are you being extracted rather than nourished?
Where are you being rewarded for abandoning yourself?
Where are you told to compete when your soul longs to connect?
Then come small refusals and silent rebellions.

Choose slowness.
Choose presence.
Choose care.

Choose to build structures around you,
that feel regenerative and fuel connection.
Do it because your nervous system knows the difference.

You do not need to overthrow the machine.
You only need to withdraw your unconscious agreement.

AARON SCOTT

Begin living a new signal.
Be the system that remembers all of life.
Be the friction in the gears of disconnection.

Be the one who steps out of the performance,
in alignment with something deeper.

No permission necessary.
Only remembrance.

When enough of us remember,
the world will shift.

Chapter 4
The Consumer Plague

The problem with consumerism goes far beyond crowded closets and maxed-out credit cards. It seeps into the way we measure our lives, quietly training us to seek meaning through what can be bought rather than what can be experienced. Consumerism draws our time, attention, and imagination toward acquisition, and in the process, our deeper needs are quietly redirected.

In doing so, it exploits our sacred longing to live with purpose, to create, and to connect with others. Consumerism hijacks that impulse and redirects it toward an object, a brand, or a persona. Products are sold for what they symbolize, not what they are. Ads sell us an emotional state such as happiness, serenity, desirability, or success. The product is the promise, the dopamine is the reward, and the cycle is endless.

Meanwhile, corporations invest billions into researching how to magnify this sense of lack. Through neuromarketing and behavioral psychology, companies use brain scans and data analytics to study what triggers our shame, what makes us feel inadequate, and what stories we will buy into. This is documented business practice.

Studies show that emotional arousal, especially fear and insecurity, can increase impulse buying and reduce brand loyalty. The more disconnected we feel from our inner worth, the more susceptible we become to manipulation. Our disconnection is deliberately engineered for profit.

Consumerism is, in many ways, a sacred impulse inverted. The human desire for beauty, connection, expression, and meaning is inherently spiritual, but in a world where matter is treated as primary and spirit as superstition, those longings are commodified and sold back to us as substitutes.

We are taught to seek transcendence in a luxury car, fulfillment in a curated lifestyle, and belonging in a logo, but these will never be sources of nourishment.

The real sickness of consumerism lies in the unspoken trade we make each day. We give our time, labor, and life force to systems that promise satisfaction yet offer only simulation. We sacrifice sacred attention for possessions that dull our presence. In doing so, we forget what fulfillment ever actually felt like.

This is a result of deep cultural conditioning. Somewhere along the way, we were taught that we are not enough and that something out there would finally complete us. But the ache inside us doesn't prove our emptiness; it highlights our misdirection.

True fulfillment comes from remembering what cannot be bought. Friendship. Stillness. Creation. Belonging. Beauty. Presence. These are not products. They are portals that lead to the very essence of a life aligned with the soul.

When we give our time back to what nourishes us, we remember that we were never empty. We were simply waiting to be filled with something real.

Consumption Culture and Religion

Consumption culture is an architecture, constructed quietly, persistently, and almost invisibly. It creeps in beneath the surface, embedded in billboards, apps, commercials, and algorithmic feeds. It thrives by keeping us distracted, slowly teaching us to assemble our identity through accumulation.

BEFORE WE FORGET

In a world where the sacred is dismissed as irrelevant, buying becomes a ritual in which acquisition replaces genuine connection. The checkout line becomes a modern altar where we seek a fleeting sense of salvation, one transaction at a time.

These rituals are engineered. People camp out overnight for new releases, often spending entire paychecks on objects that offer only the illusion of fulfillment. Their sacrifices appear sacred, but only because the system mistakes urgency for importance and ownership for meaning.

The market persuades us that we are expressing ourselves through what we buy, but more often, we are simply performing. When our worth is tied to brands, we begin to lease identity and rent belonging from systems that profit from our insecurity. We are not simply buying things. We are trying to buy ourselves back. We reach outward for meaning we think we lack, trying to fill the quiet ache that whispers, *You are not enough*. And the more we perform, the further we drift from who we truly are beneath the charade.

When our identity is separated from our inner truth, brands take on a symbolic meaning. They become modern talismans meant to signal status, tribe, or desirability. Logos and labels are treated as signs of success, beauty, and power.

As with all distortions, we begin to live from the outside in. We stop asking what is meaningful and start asking what will be seen. Image overtakes truth. As brands become belief systems and marketing becomes mythology, we start worshiping the symbols of life instead of life itself.

We embrace the machine's substitute religion because it offers predictability and rhythm through rituals that give us something to hold onto. Yet at its core, there is no divinity to be found, only endless displays of absence.

None of this is about rejecting material things. It's an invitation to break the spell of consumerism. To reclaim our sovereignty, we must recognize how our meaning has been outsourced to what can be purchased and displayed. To reclaim ourselves from the marketplace, we must remember that what we seek has never lived in a product. It lives in presence, in inner alignment, and in the sacred memory of truth.

We are here to remember that what truly nourishes us cannot be bought.

Excess Trauma

As a society we have come to mistake excess for abundance, and in doing so, we have forgotten the essence of what it means to live in sufficiency. True abundance is the quiet recognition that life provides what we need when we are in alignment with it. It moves through the current of mutual care. Through knowing that what is offered will be replenished. Abundance nourishes the body and soul because it harmonizes with the sacred rhythms of life itself.

Excess, in its purest sense, is abundance distorted. It is a sign of the personal trauma we have endured through systems that tell us to search for meaning in what we can possess rather than who we are. It grows out of the disorientation that comes when we forget our connection to the greater web of life. Excess is one of the clearest symptoms of our cultural conditioning. It offers tangible evidence of a mind trained to believe disconnection is normal.

We long for excess because something within us aches to be soothed. When we peel back our longing layers, what we find is an anxious accumulation of objects meant to pacify an emptiness that refuses to be filled. The trauma of excess reveals itself as our reflex to buy, upgrade, decorate, and consume; anything to quiet the void that surfaces when we stop.

Excess is a performance of wealth that disguises a poverty of meaning.

The more severed we become from our true essence, the more we reach for substitutes. We hoard experiences, objects, and identities, believing that if we just keep adding, the hollow center will eventually disappear. But it doesn't. It deepens. And the more we consume unconsciously, the more we amplify the very emptiness we are trying to escape. It illuminates our collective spiritual malnutrition.

We have normalized this pathology. We call it success. We call it hustle. We call it living our best life. However, behind the curated images, a quiet epidemic of nervous system dysregulation, burnout, comparison fatigue, and inner disorientation persists. Children are handed screens instead of touch. Teenagers are taught to brand themselves before they ever understand who they are. Adults are celebrated for their productivity and dismissed when they pause. The notion of sufficiency becomes hard to grasp.

This, in truth, is an unspoken war on presence.

Excess teaches us to bypass the inner world entirely. It says, *Don't feel. Don't listen. Don't stop.* Instead of tending to the ache, we pile more on top of it. *Don't sit with your pain. Buy something instead. Follow the trend.* So we rush, we reach, we perform, yet what we are truly missing is the capacity to be with ourselves again.

Healing begins when we recognize the noise as nothing more than a distraction from the wound. It begins when we can say with quiet clarity, *I have enough. I am enough. I don't need more to be more.*

This is about reconnecting and reclaiming a state of sufficiency that capitalism tells us doesn't exist. When we realize that the feeling of insufficiency was externally manufactured, we begin to untangle ourselves from the trance. We remember that what we were seeking was never out there to begin with.

Objectification and Self-Branding

In the modern world, consumerism and objectification feed the same distortion. Consumerism teaches us to measure worth by what can be displayed or bought. Objectification teaches us to measure worth by how something looks or how it can be used. As a result, everything becomes an object. We reduce people to profiles to swipe, scroll, and evaluate. We judge relationships by their utility. We carefully filter our emotions so they will be acceptable to others. We even treat ourselves as something to package and improve.

Once this reduction takes hold, consumerism feeds on it. A world that defines value by what can be bought, sold, or displayed trains us to measure ourselves the same way. A child who learns to equate worth with performance becomes an adult who buys the products that promise to enhance that performance. A teenager who scrutinizes their body becomes a consumer primed for industries that thrive on body dissatisfaction. Objectification supplies the gaze, and consumerism sells the cure. Together they form a loop that never resolves, because the sense of lack they create is the very fuel that keeps the machine running.

This training begins almost as soon as we can speak. Children learn quickly that their worth is defined by how they look, what they achieve, and how others respond to them. The lessons are subtle. A smile earns approval from a parent, while a tantrum brings shame. In school, they are rewarded for efficiency and compliance, and dismissed when they wander or rest.

Over time, these lessons sink in. What begins as the judgments of parents, teachers, and peers becomes the voice inside our own heads. We learn to watch ourselves the way others once watched us. Without realizing it, we become our own monitor. We scrutinize our reflection in the mirror. We gauge our output by what earns approval. We scroll and compare, even when no one is telling us to. Slowly, our bodies become projects to improve, our personalities become content to perform, and our worth becomes a score to manage. The soul, which cannot be measured or marketed, fades quietly into the background.

And the way we treat ourselves naturally becomes the way we treat others. The fragmentation within spills outward until our vision of others fractures too. We no longer meet people as they are. We meet them as roles to fill, functions to serve, and mirrors for our own needs.

Culture reinforces this gaze. We are trained to see one another through the same lens we use for products. Women are grossly objectified, reduced to items to be consumed. Advertisements and films train us to look at their bodies before hearing their voices, while social media platforms reward desirability with clicks and follows. Men, meanwhile, are valued by their ability to produce or provide. A man who cannot display strength, wealth, or status is treated as less. The sacred dance between polarities is flattened into a marketplace of roles, where worth is assigned by what can be shown and sold.

Even our labor is objectified. Work is no longer an expression of calling. It is flattened into a sterile metric of productivity or a badge of social legitimacy. You are not asked if your work brings joy, but if it advances your career. A child is not asked what makes them feel alive, but "What do you want to be?" The question itself pushes them to translate their being into a marketable role, preparing them to measure their life by titles and outputs rather than inner aliveness.

Capitalism, especially in its late-stage form, carries this logic to its extreme. Beauty is airbrushed and sold back to us in jars and creams. Rest is packaged into retreats and sleep apps. Even authenticity is performed. We sell our emotions as content on feeds. We sell versions of ourselves to gain attention, forgetting that who we are cannot be owned or performed.

And when everything is a product, nothing is sacred. The more we consume, the more we learn to see the world in terms of consumption. The more we objectify ourselves and others, the harder it becomes to recognize what is real. Amid all the scrolling, branding, and producing, we hollow out. We begin to forget the taste of unmeasured joy, the stillness that steadies us, and the depth of presence no market can touch.

Waking Up

We don't awaken in this age by rejecting the material; we do so by dethroning it. We must shift our focus to what gives life genuine meaning. Awakening invites this clarity. It allows us to stop outsourcing our identity to possessions and begin listening to the voice beneath the noise that says, *You are already whole.*

In this culture, awakening is a radical act. It says, *I will no longer be defined by the system. I will remember who I am without needing anything outside of me to prove it.*

Ask yourself, *What do I own that is owning me? What part of me is performing instead of living? What am I afraid will disappear if I stop chasing, scrolling, or upgrading? Who am I without the things I buy?*

These questions open doorways, inviting us to slip past the facade of the false self and find our way back to what is real. They whisper of a home we have never truly left, where belonging is not something to earn but something inherent to life itself.

Your true freedom comes from simply knowing that you are already enough, here and now, in your sacred uniqueness. You don't need to prove anything because you know your worth is not conditional. To awaken is to take back what has been hidden, to meet yourself fully in presence and to treat sufficiency as sacred. When you awaken, you feel the pulse of life moving through you, constant and unbroken, beneath all the distractions. It's always been there waiting for you to claim it.

When you live this way, the endless search grinds to a halt. You are carried by a sacred current that cannot be bought. You stand unshaken in a world that profits from your instability. You are no longer available to the system that feeds on emptiness because you carry sufficiency within you.

Building the New Dream

If we are to evolve and build a conscious civilization, we must first dismantle the illusion that our worth comes from consumption. We must become brave enough to imagine a world no longer built on microtrends and monetized attention, but rooted in the deeper architecture of what actually makes life worth living.

We must remember the sacred pulse that flows through our bodies, nature, and the endless sky above us. It reminds us that life was always a relationship, never a transaction, and that we are here to take part in a living sacred exchange.

A conscious world rises when we honor the holiness of the ordinary. It grows when we meet each moment with integrity. It holds when we restore depth to our relationships, meaning to our work, and tenderness to the ways we touch one another's lives.

BEFORE WE FORGET

An awakened world comes when we raise children who know how to meet their emotions without running to a screen to numb them, when we praise them for feeling deeply, for wondering fully, and for speaking their truth even when it shakes them. It endures when we teach them to trust the compass within rather than chase the shallow applause of a world that cannot see them.

This is the dream that belongs to us. It is a vision of homes that shelter the spirit rather than display status, of schools that guard curiosity as a sacred flame rather than flatten it into obedience, and of communities bound by presence instead of excess.

It begins when we create more than we consume, when we listen more than we broadcast, when we live from coherence rather than image.

This dream cannot be packaged or sold. It cannot be marketed back to us in fragments. It's not a product. It's a remembering, and it waits, steady and alive, for us to choose it.

Our Meditation

> Consumerism has metastasized into a worldview.
> It trains us to see the world as a storehouse of things to acquire, upgrade, and discard.
>
> In this story, the measure of a life is its external display:
> how much you have collected, curated, and performed.
>
> We forget that this is relatively new for humanity.
> For most of our existence, value was relational,
> measured in belonging.
>
> Now, we measure it in transactions.
> Even our identities are marketed back to us,
> as if who we are were just another lifestyle brand in the making.

AARON SCOTT

But meaning has never been a product.
It is a practice.
It is cultivated in the soil of relationships,
in the slow weaving of presence over time.

It emerges in the moments no one can package:
a shared glance,
a deep breath on a cool summer night,
a sudden laugh that cannot be planned or sold.

When we begin to see consumerism as part of the machine that runs on our longing,
we realize our greatest act of resistance is refusal.
Refusing to measure ourselves by our possessions.
Refusing to believe that something new will always be better.
Refusing to give our soul away for the next dopamine hit of acquisition.

The cure is to return beauty to its rightful place,
as a living conversation between the self, the living world, and the Divine.

Stepping out of the consumerist trance is to remember
that what we hunger for most cannot be bought,
and that the most valuable things we will ever hold
are the ones we cannot own.

Part Two
The Unraveling

Chapter 5
Fearing the Truth

Awakening is often romanticized. We imagine it as a moment of illumination, a blissful breakthrough where everything clicks into place and life becomes clear. We picture mountain vistas, spiritual epiphanies, and a newfound peace that carries us above the noise of the world.

But real awakening is rarely so cinematic. It's not always a light. Sometimes, it begins as a collapse. A disintegration. A slow unthreading of the life we once believed was real. This is because that life was built on stories that no longer make sense.

True awakening reveals illusions. It strips us. It pulls away the inherited roles, identities, and narratives we once depended on for a sense of self. It peels back the scaffolding we mistook for reality, exposing a raw and trembling truth. Much of what we were taught to consider normal was founded on fear, performance, and engineering.

People don't resist awakening because they're ignorant. They resist because truth shakes the very structures that once held them together. It pulls at the beliefs they have mistaken for truths, the ones through which they have built their sense of self. Awakening is about shedding the inherited beliefs that were never truly ours and then asking us to stand in the unfamiliar without a script. It invites us into the terrifying grace of uncertainty.

At the psychological level, this feels like losing your identity. At the somatic level, it can feel like danger. The nervous system, wired for survival, often interprets awakening as a threat because what is familiar, even if harmful, feels safer than what is unknown.

Culturally, awakening threatens conformity. Entire systems are built on illusions that require collective participation. When someone begins to see through them, they disrupt the equilibrium. They are often dismissed as naive, unstable, or extreme, but what they are really doing is refusing to participate in someone else's game. And that refusal, especially when embodied with clarity, becomes revolutionary.

This is why real awakening isn't always joyful. It's often messy, slow, and isolating. It can feel like grief, like disorientation, like standing at the edge of a cliff with no map and no familiar ground to return to.

And yet, when it is embraced, it offers deep clarity and sustainable freedom. This isn't the kind of freedom that grants us wings to float above the world looking down on life from above, but rather the kind that grants us the opportunity to live consciously, rooted in truth, in our lived reality with presence. Through the journey of awakening, we are reintroduced to the version of ourselves that has been buried under a lifetime of delusion and distraction. We get to see what is real, and we get to remove everything that is not. It's not so difficult to see then why a journey that offers so much is kept to the margins even by those who need what it offers the most. Yet it's equally easy to see why humanity eventually evolves through awakening because it is anchored in one tenet, and that is truth. And whenever truth is up against illusion, it cannot be defeated.

Ego Death

The ego is a survival strategy, and it is best not to look at it as a villain. It forms in early life, piece by piece, as a way to make sense of the world, to stay safe, and to feel seen. It gives us a name, a role, a story. It organizes experience and creates identity to help us belong. In that way, the ego is sacred. It is scaffolding for the soul, but scaffolding is meant to be temporary.

BEFORE WE FORGET

When awakening begins, it is an invitation to see beyond the barriers imposed by the ego. However, to the ego, that invitation feels like death. The ego has spent its entire life building structure, weaving stories about who we are, what we must do to be loved, and where we fit in the world. Awakening threatens those very structures. It peels away falsehoods and says gently, or not, "You are more than this."

To the ego, this feels like falling, like chaos, so it clings. It fights for continuity. It panics. It scrambles to regain control. It rebrands. It performs spiritual identity. It says, *I am the one who is awake now,* because it is afraid of being nothing at all.

This is why so much of the awakening process feels like disorientation, because something that we took to be complete truth is revealing itself as falsehood. The roles, titles, personas, and performances no longer feel real. The center collapses. The old self can no longer hold. That collapse is the beginning of the return to reality.

Just as with all other illusions that we have depended on for our identity, the ego simply needs to be reoriented from the driver to the passenger. It has been an imposter reigning as the master, and it's time to demote it to a servant of the whole self. It can and will still help us function, organize, and navigate, but it no longer needs to define all of who we are.

However, full integration only comes when we stop resisting the death of the egoic illusion. When we let the ego grieve what it thought it had to be. When we allow the disintegration of the ego to be holy, our heartbreak to be sacred, and the unraveling to be honored.

This is why our gentleness is crucial, and why anchoring ourselves in truth matters. This is why breath work, conscious ritual, and embodiment practices matter. These practices are not meant to engulf your entire being, as this will yield another illusory adaptation, not better or worse. Living fully in an overextended manner, no matter the polarity, will create the same fragmentation, only in a different flavor. The evolution of humanity is about balance, reciprocity, and right relationship with all aspects of our identity and our lives.

But in the end take solace in knowing that you are not losing yourself. You are simply shedding the version of yourself that was never whole to begin with. And in that loss, something real emerges. Something that does not need to be paraded around, classified, or even validated to exist. Something that is simply, quiet, rooted and ultimately unshakable.

This is the soul reclaiming its rightful seat at the head of the table.

The Body is Your Compass

Awakening is often viewed as solely a mental or spiritual process, but without the body, it cannot hold. Without the nervous system, it will not last. Awakening may begin in the mind, but it is the body that must sustain it. And that is where things often unravel.

To the rational mind, truth can feel exhilarating, but to the nervous system, truth can feel dangerous. This is biology. The body is wired to prioritize safety above expansion. It seeks the familiar, even when the familiar is painful. The unknown, even when beautiful, registers as a threat.

This is why a person may continue returning to a toxic relationship that diminishes them, or a habit that slowly erodes their well-being. Logically, they may know it's harmful. But to their nervous system, the pain is predictable. It carries the cold comforting illusion of control. A new path, even one that promises healing or joy, can overwhelm the body's internal alarm bells.

The body doesn't care if the disruption comes from trauma or from awakening. It only senses that something is changing. And for a system built on pattern recognition, change is danger. This means that even the most liberating insight can cause the body to contract.

This is why so many people experience a spiritual breakthrough followed by a collapse, a moment of expansion followed by shutdown. It is survival. The body is doing what it was designed to do. It is instinctively pulling you back to what is known, back to the script, back to the illusion that once kept you safe.

This may manifest as anxiety or numbness. You may notice resistance, dissociation, cravings, or emotional volatility. These are signs that your system is trying to protect you from what it cannot yet understand. This isn't some gauge of validity, but rather a warning of imminent change.

If our awakening is to take root, we must welcome the body to the party. This is a gentle reeducation, a slow, sacred unlearning. The body must be shown over time that it is safe to see clearly. That your personal evolution and expansion do not mean annihilation.

The body must learn to breathe in a new rhythm. In the Divine rhythm. The reeducation here is to orient to presence, move with curiosity instead of fear, and to soften the grip on the old story. This is slow work, brave work; it is the holiest work you will ever do. Its curriculum is breath work, conscious movement, stillness, and finding safety in relationships. This coursework speaks to the child within and says, "You are not being destroyed. You are coming home."

When this process is regulated, the body becomes a bridge between spirit and form. It becomes the ground on which truth can resurface. And when the body trusts that it will not be abandoned or overridden, it begins to stay. The nervous system holds the memory of every story you have outgrown, and it also holds the possibility of a new one. This new story is one where you do not have to choose between expansion and safety, and where you are allowed to grow without leaving yourself behind.

Feeling Returns

Our modern life is designed to keep us fragmented and numb. We rarely notice it, but it is the common thread. Endless content. Constant urgency. Curated identities. Spirituality stripped of depth and repackaged for convenience. Beneath it all we are told, "Do not feel too much." "Do not look too closely." "Just keep going."

Awakening disrupts this unconscious trance. It reopens the inner world and breaks the spell of mental and emotional dissociation. It brings forward what was silenced. When we welcome this evolution, the armor that once helped us survive begins to soften, and we start to feel again.

This is often the most unexpected part of awakening. We grieve. We rage. We tremble. We remember what it meant to be small and scared. We feel shame that was never ours to carry. We feel joy that was long muted. We feel sorrow for what we did not protect. And for many of us, we feel this for the first time in years.

We grieve for the world, for the pain we once ignored, and for the suffering we now cannot unsee. We mourn the parts of ourselves that had to disappear to fit in. We feel rage toward the systems and stories that taught us to suppress the very things that make us human. We feel sorrow for the identities we built and now must shed.

Do not mistake this emotional flood as a detour, or worse a derailing. It is the path itself. However, it can feel overwhelming, especially for those who were never shown how to hold their emotions with care. When the floodgates open, it can feel like drowning, because we have never been taught to welcome them in.

Don't fall victim to bypass here as real awakening demands presence. It does not ask for spiritual performance. It does not rush you. It does not fix you. It invites you to sit with what is raw, to breathe with what is heavy, and to hold what aches without collapsing.

This return of feeling is your divine restoration. The pain that rises was always there. It lived beneath the image you projected, beneath the tasks you completed, and beneath the synthetic smile you wore when your soul was exhausted from distortion. There is a holiness in unraveling, a sacredness in the sob you cannot explain, because, in that moment, you are no longer performing, you are fostering your truth.

Awakening returns us to the full experience of being alive. It snaps us out of the hypnosis of living solely through habit and reaction. And in that space, we remember that inner alignment is a way of being we can choose time and time again.

Truth Disrupts

We are, all of us, drawn to certainty. Predictability feels like safety and control promises us that if we follow the right steps, speak the right words, and live the right way, life will reward us with stability and success. This is another seduction of illusion. It offers simplicity that is attractive. The inherent problem here is that meaning cannot be mastered, and mystery cannot be mapped. These misunderstood concepts are in many ways the missteps of a young civilization's attempt to institutionalize the sacred. To attempt to control the Divine is a sort of naivete of a desperate egoic mind.

For a while, this illusion works. It provides a script, it keeps us insulated, and it allows us to feel prepared in a world that feels too vast and too unpredictable to fully grasp. But awakening disrupts that illusion. It takes away the structures we mistook for truth and leaves us with something raw, alive, and more difficult to define.

Awakening reveals that life cannot and was never meant to be reduced to a formula. Or even worse, that humanity was never meant to be governed by industrial logic reinforced by institutions. Awakening shows us that the healing does not arrive on schedule and that purpose is not something you achieve. And when that revelation is truly accepted and digested, something deeper begins to shift. The narratives we depended on begin to lose their grip. The roles we performed begin to feel hollow, and the systems we trusted reveal their cracks. This propels us to question everything.

This is the foray into our lived truth. We see clearly that truth is not a fixed point, and clearly not dogma. Our truth is alive, ever changing, and intimate. It breathes. This sacred vitality threatens the part of us that has built identity through control. The ego wants to organize reality the way we have been indoctrinated to construct our lives: into a grid, a checklist, or a fixed map. It wants guarantees.

Truth here invites a different sort of relationship. It does not seek domination, but rather asks us to listen, to soften, and to allow the unknown to arrive without forcing it into shape.

So, awakening becomes a kind of disorientation. A stripping away. What once seemed obvious now feels uncertain. What once felt safe begins to feel constricting. It is like standing barefoot at the edge of the ocean at night. You cannot see where the tide ends. You cannot predict what is coming, but something in you knows this is where real life begins.

In this space, there is no script, no certainty, and certainly no prewritten outcome. What begins to emerge is not a new belief or another constricting system. What emerges is simply a direction and an invitation to an open conversation. No doctrine, no rigid instruction, no superficial ritual required. You are being asked to be true to yourself, and equally important, you are being asked to be real. And what does this request grant you? It gifts you a return to your own clarity and ultimately your sovereignty.

Why? Because you are no longer navigating the world from the outside in. You are beginning to live from the inside out. From presence. From truth. From the part of you that no longer needs validation to feel real.

Truth, in this form, is relational. It lives in your capacity to trust what you know, even when you cannot yet explain it.

This is the truth that heals. But to reach it, the frame must break and the illusions must fall apart.

Truth Questions Belonging

Even though we have been led to shape our current consciousness around external disconnection and internal fragmentation, we enter the world trying to shape ourselves around connection. As children, our survival depends on food and shelter, but it also depends on being seen, accepted, and included. We learn quickly which parts of ourselves are welcomed and which are too much. We adapt. We mold. We trade authenticity for attachment.

Belonging becomes the blueprint, and with it comes a set of quiet agreements. We are instructed to speak a certain way, believe in certain things, and are told what is unacceptable. These formative agreements shape our identity, because they provide what we are seeking. They help us stay connected. Out of necessity, and not necessarily resonance, we absorb beliefs about God, gender, race, morality, and success. We carry them for years, sometimes our whole lives, without realizing they were never ours to begin with.

Then something shifts. Sometimes, this shift happens slowly, through lived experience. Sometimes, it occurs suddenly, through loss, rupture, or awakening. A quiet discomfort begins to rise. We start to notice where the story no longer fits. The faith we inherited begins to feel hollow. The culture we worked so hard to belong to starts to feel shallow. What once provided meaning now raises questions we can no longer ignore.

To see the truth is one thing. To live it is another.

Truth asks for courage. And courage, in this context, often comes at a cost. It may mean risking the very belonging we were conditioned to protect. The relationships built around shared illusion. The communities that depend on silence. Oftentimes, the approval that was never anchored in who we really are.

This is why truth destabilizes the agreements we have spent a lifetime maintaining. Speaking it will often bring judgment, isolation, even exile. It can bring being labeled ungrateful, rebellious, difficult, or naive. It can bring becoming a stranger in rooms that once felt like home.

But false belonging brings connections built on performance. It is not the same as love. Awakening will eventually ask us to choose between inclusion and integrity.

The grief that follows is real. We mourn the version of ourselves that tried so hard to keep synthetic relationships intact. We feel the ache of self-abandonment, the years spent hiding, editing, and shrinking to stay within reach of something that could never see us fully.

But this grief is yet another gateway.

What awaits on the other side of that rupture is a different kind of belonging, one built on resonance and truth. This belonging arises from being known, not acceptable.

This is the slow beauty of awakening. As we shed the roles we once played to be loved, we begin to attract relationships where love does not require performance. We find people who meet us in our clarity, who recognize us beyond the mask, and who do not ask us to shrink in order to stay.

Even before these external relationships arrive, a deeper sense of belonging begins to take root. A real belonging to your self, to your body, to your Earth, and to the Divine. Your place here cannot be given or revoked by anyone else because it is no longer transactional. It is knowing that you are true to yourself, even when that truth costs you something.

This is not an easy path. To speak the truth in a world that punishes honesty is a radical act. To keep loving in a world that rewards performance is a sacred one.

Awakening will ask you to be loyal to the part of you that knows. Even when others do not understand. Even when it is lonely. Even when it shakes the ground you once stood on. Because the belonging that matters most is the kind that calls you home.

Systems Depend on Illusions

The illusions we are conditioned to live within are embedded in the structures that shape our lives. Economic systems, organized religion, education, and media are not passive. They sustain particular beliefs about value, identity, and power, and they do so by training us to accept illusion as reality.

Capitalism, in its current overextended form, sells us the idea that productivity equals worth, that our accumulation means safety, and that our fulfillment can be purchased. It rewards our exhaustion and calls it ambition. It convinces us that our deepest longings can be satisfied with upgrades, promotions, or more things.

Religion, in its most distorted form, no longer offers direct communion with the Divine. It replaces presence with authority. Life's mystery becomes accepted doctrine, and your inner knowing becomes institutional hierarchy. Your spiritual longing is redirected into your obedience. And most diabolical of all, your salvation is cheapened into a transaction.

Education, instead of sparking curiosity or critical thought, trains our compliance. It teaches students what to think rather than how to feel their way into their personal truth. It rewards our repetition and it grooms us for performance. Eventually, it conditions us to look outward for authority rather than inward for clarity.

Media is designed to influence. It's an industry after all. And it's through the potency of its influence that it can monetize your attention. It floods our senses with urgency, fear, and distraction. It demands our attention and promotes noise. If overindulged unconsciously, it will fracture our coherence and corral us further into a manufactured reality built on stimulation and control.

When we awaken within these systems we acknowledge how deeply we have internalized them. We have given them sanctuary in our nervous system, in our desires, in our emotional patterns, and in the very language we use to define our reality.

Our awakening within systems that depend on our sleep makes us a disturbance. And when we question what we inherited we loosen the grip of everything built on our forgetting.

We will never change these systems by mirroring their distortions. We change them by becoming something else entirely. We change them through conscious disengagement, by returning to what is true and building from that place.

All of these illusions are fragile. They survive only when we perform for them. When we stop performing and start remembering, the structure begins to shake, simply because we stop feeding the machine distortion.

This is cellular truth. The systems that depend on distortion lose power the moment we reclaim our own. And when enough people stop obeying illusion, the world begins to reorder itself around what is real.

Threshold Doorways

Awakening unfolds at the speed of sincerity. But, as we have come to understand, when illusions dissolve, the body can interpret that unraveling as chaos. These doorways are simple gestures to help you stay present in the disorientation.

Begin where you are. Let it be enough.

1. Anchor Yourself Through Rituals

Awakening often strips away what once felt stable. The illusions may fall quickly, but the soul still needs something steady to rest in. This is where rituals become your anchor. Choose simple acts and infuse them with presence. Light a candle mindfully before your nighttime routine. Take a conscious breath before you respond. They don't need to be grand. In fact, let them be small. Let them be sacred. When you practice with intention, rituals become a thread that reconnects you to what is real.

2. Listen to Your Body

Truth cannot land in a body that feels unsafe. Your nervous system must learn that awakening does not mean danger. Begin with your body. Press your feet gently into the floor. Inhale into the softness of your belly. Rest a hand on your chest. Stretch. Walk slowly. Let your body know it belongs. Ask your body what it needs. Then listen. You are seeding your garden. Your regulation is the soil where awakening takes root.

3. Feed Your Curiosity

Your mind will reach for answers. Your ego will demand clarity. But your truth does not come through control. When your discomfort rises, meet it with curiosity. Ask yourself, *What part of me is trying to protect me right now? What fear is asking to be seen?* Let yourself wonder without rushing toward a resolution. Let your questions breathe. You don't need to fix or analyze. You only need to make room for what wants to emerge. Wonder softens your armor. It invites your truth to rise without force.

4. Be Seen by Another
We are not meant to awaken alone. Some truths are too tender to carry in silence. Share your process with someone who can witness you without needing to fix you. Let your voice be heard without some grand performance. Reveal with pride who you are. If no one is available, speak aloud to yourself. Record what you are feeling. Write it down. The soul relaxes when it feels welcomed.

5. Welcome the Unknown
Truth is not always clear at first. Sometimes, it arrives as space. Sometimes, it only speaks through your silence. Sit in that space. Let your questions remain unanswered. Let your insight arrive in its own time. You don't need to chase it. You don't need to grasp at anything. Mystery is sacred. It is in your pause where your deeper knowing begins to form.

6. Accept Your Fears
Your fear will rise when your truth begins to shake the walls of what is familiar. Do not silence it. Do not override it. Sit with it. Speak to it gently. Say, *I know you are trying to protect me. Thank you, but I am ready to let something deeper guide me now.* When your fear is acknowledged, it softens. When you stop running from it, it no longer needs to chase you. It's your relationship with fear that's the enemy. Use your fear as another tool in your toolkit.

7. Embrace What Leaves You
As your old beliefs, identities, and roles fall away, take a moment to mark their departure. Write a letter to what is leaving. Throw it in the garbage. Bury it. Offer a prayer. Say quietly, *"Thank you for what you gave me. I am moving forward."* Your grief and your gratitude can walk together. What dies makes space for what is real. Sanctify their departure.

AARON SCOTT

Our Meditation

There is no right way to awaken.
No map that will lead you step by step.
No spiritual milestone to prove you have arrived.

There is only your own deepening.
The way your breath catches when your truth brushes against you.
The way your body shakes when everything in you wants to brace,
yet you choose to soften.
The way you stay when illusion tells you to run.

Awakening is something you allow.
Your truth is already inside you,
pressing from beneath the surface,
waiting for the moment you stop resisting long enough to let it rise.

When it does,
you will feel it in your bones.
Your jaw will loosen.
Your tears will flow.
Your breath will deepen.

So breathe with it.
Let your hands tremble.
Let the illusions go.
Let your questions remain unanswered.

You are not lost here.
You are between masks.
And you are closer than you think to your true self.

From here, you live with the raw,
steady pulse of sincerity.
You begin to walk again,
basking in your truth.

BEFORE WE FORGET

When you awaken, you feel everything that your sight reveals.

The illusions that once suffocated you begin to fade.
The roles you played slip away.
The institutions you once clutched feel hollow.
Even the image you spent years constructing
begins to constrict the life now moving through you.

Yet life does not stop.
Bills still arrive.
Children still need dinner.
The clock still ticks.
Awakening comes without a sabbatical.

So you learn to walk between worlds.
Too awake to return to the old.
Too unsteady to fully inhabit the new.
Wanting to live in truth
but unsure how to stay intact while doing it.

You do not need to rush.
You only need to stay.

Because surviving inside your awakening is the sacred resilience.
It is proof that you are building the muscle to carry more truth.
And it is from this ground
that a new world begins to take shape.

Chapter 6
Keeping It Real

Few talk about what it is like to wake up in a world that does not change with you. You begin to see through the illusion, but the illusion still expects you to play along.

Your soul expands, but your life goes on. You are standing in your truth while surrounded by structures that depend on your forgetting. It is disorienting, even painful, to remember who you are in a culture that keeps asking you to perform who you are not.

This stretch, the space between inner awakening and outer integration, is where many falter, because awakening disrupts the agreements that once held their world together. What you used to tolerate now feels intolerable. What once passed as normal now stings with distortion.

But this discomfort is the heart of transformation. To awaken and still show up inside the dream is one of the most courageous things a human being can do.

Living Between Worlds

Awakening gives you new eyes. You begin to see through the systems, and the stories that once upheld them start to unravel. What once felt solid begins to crumble. What once passed as normal begins to feel deeply unnatural.

However, the world around you does not change just because you do. It keeps moving. It keeps asking you to play along. You sit in meetings while your soul aches for meaning. You engage in small talk while harboring quiet revelations. You scroll through distractions that no longer soothe. You laugh when you want to cry. You show up, but you no longer fit in.

This is the space between the dream and the dawn. The old no longer holds, but the new has not fully arrived. You are too awake to pretend, too embedded to walk away, too changed to go back, too early for others to understand. It can feel like exile, even like floating.

There is grief in this liminal space. Grief for what no longer feels true. Grief for the roles you outgrew. Grief for the ways you once belonged. You feel the beauty in moments others overlook. You feel the ache in conversations that scream performance. You begin to care differently. More deeply. More quietly. More honestly.

The task now is to remain awake within the dream. To breathe truth into places where distortion was taught. To walk gently with compassion. To remember that others are still sleeping because they are not ready.

You are now a bridge between paradigms, rooted in what is real, moving through what is false, and planting seeds for what is next. You are now a sacred medicine for a dis-eased world. You are a sacred offering. And while it may stretch you, it is shaping you into someone who can hold both the light and the weight of awakening.

A New Sensitivity

Awakening returns you to feeling. The numbness begins to lift. What once passed as background noise now echoes through your entire being. The joy of a stranger's laughter. The ache behind someone's passing glance. The hunger in someone's eyes as they rush past you.

You start to feel it all, from the whispers within your heart to the pulse of the collective field around you. You feel the sorrow of the world and the fatigue of systems too heavy to sustain life. Your body becomes more porous. The walls that once kept you separate begin to dissolve. What felt like strength reveals itself as suppression, and what looked like coping now seems like hiding.

This sensitivity is evidence that your humanity is returning. But it can feel like too much. You cry at music, at light, at the space between words. You feel joy and grief in the same breath. You wake with a heart full of ache and awe. You move through life with your skin turned inward. It's overwhelming, but it is sacred.

The world won't understand you right away. Don't forget, it rewards detachment. It demands you to manage, to produce, to perform, but you have outgrown its marching orders. You have returned to the deeper rhythm, and that rhythm carries a different demand. It asks you to stay open. To stay soft. To feel without drowning.

To survive with this sensitivity, you must build new practices of care. Rest is no longer optional. Silence is no longer a luxury. You must learn to create a haven for your own tenderness. To anchor your body, to protect your peace, and to pause when the noise becomes too loud.

This sensitivity, when held with care, becomes your strength. It becomes your intuition, your compassion, and your sacred vision. It becomes the bridge between the soul and the world. It reminds you that your softness is the beginning of your healing.

You are falling into your truth, and truth, when it enters the body, feels like sensation. It feels like love. And you are learning how to carry it.

The Last Act

Awakening often dismantles the identity you once depended on because it was built for performance and survival.

You inherited roles. You shaped yourself around approval. You became who you needed to be to feel safe, to feel wanted, and to feel worthy. You were assigned identities: achiever, outsider, caretaker, rebel. Over time, these became your architecture and you built your identity around what the world rewarded.

But the soul doesn't care about cheap rewards. It longs for authenticity. It wants you to embrace your truth.

So, the roles begin to feel hollow, and your acts grow exhausting. Your script starts to lose its allure, and your prior performances now feel difficult to reenact.

At first, you may try to adjust the mask, tweak the costume, and return to the role with a new approach. But something deeper has already shifted. The scaffolding has already buckled and your voice inside says, *This isn't me.*

This is a terrifying realization because, if you are not who you have always been, then who are you now? The answer to this ache arrives as silence and as something unknown.

This is the unraveling before your reformation. The moment when you stand naked in your own life, unsure of how to speak, how to move, and generally how to be.

You are shedding what was never truly yours.

To survive this passage, you must resist the impulse to reconstruct too quickly. Let the in-between be sacred. Let the ambiguity be honored. There's nothing to rush here. Instead, you simply need to listen, to rest, and to let what is real emerge without force.

This is counter-intuitive to how you have historically lived your life. Everything you have done to curate yourself previously has been through concerted effort. Through training, through conforming, and through performing. Let the old blueprint fade away. It's not the sacred one. Your authenticity will emerge.

Choosing to Stay

Accepting truth can be extremely liberating, but truth does not seek to comfort you. It seeks your authentic alignment. It takes what you have been indoctrinated with, how you have betrayed yourself, and what you have learned to tolerate and it blasts it over your internal loudspeaker.

There will be days when awakening feels like too much. When your clarity feels more like a burden than a gift, when your sensitivity feels raw and unrelenting, and when you wonder if returning to sleep would be easier than holding this much truth.

You may miss the comfort of not knowing. You may envy those who still fit inside the story you have outgrown. You may look at the chaos of the world and whisper to yourself, "*I did not ask for this.*"

And still, you stay.

You keep breathing. You keep waking. You keep choosing to return to presence, because it is honest. Because the cost of abandoning yourself again is higher than the cost of staying.

Keeping it real is not glamorous. It's not always expansive. Often, it's quiet. Often, it's slow. It's a kind of devotion that goes unseen, a practice of remaining open even when the world feels too much to bear.

It looks like sitting with your truth when silence would be more polite. Feeling your grief when numbness would be more convenient. Pausing to breathe when the culture demands performance. It's returning to yourself when everything around you pulls you away.

Staying means holding onto your softness without forcing yourself to push harder. It asks that you remain resilient and remember what truly matters when everything else around you has forgotten.

You stay because something inside, something deeper than explanation, has aligned with your soul. This sacred resonance scoffs at external validation because you don't have anything to prove anymore.

This is what survival looks like now. It's your steady return to what cannot be taken, along a path charted by your soul.

AARON SCOTT

Our Meditation

Surviving while awakening is not a flaw in your path.
You are not failing because you feel tired or overwhelmed.

You are not broken.
You are not lost.
You are not separate.

You are rejoining the Divine rhythm that moves through all of life.

This process will shake you.
It will pull the breath from your chest.
It will make the ground shake beneath your feet.

You are not alone.
There are countless others moving through their days,
clocking in, caring for children, making small talk,
while their inner world rearranges itself in silence.

We were meant to be held during this kind of becoming.
But in a world of deadlines, algorithms, and illusions,
the container must be built from within.

Let your discomfort speak.
Let your breath anchor you when your mind begins to spin.
Let beauty steady you when you forget what is real.

You need only one voice that says, "I feel it too."

Silence can be sacred.
Distance can be a medicine.

When your life begins to echo your truth,
something will shift.

BEFORE WE FORGET

It's not your insight that changes you.
It's your capacity to hold your truth without shattering.

Awakening finds footing in clarity.
And that clarity is calling you home.

Chapter 7
Mask Off

The systems you were taught to trust have conditioned you to identify with roles, titles, even pain. When the house of cards collapses, what remains?

Modern society has taught us to trust in its systems as the guiding pillars of truth, order, and meaning. But what if those very systems, while once intended to serve, have slowly conditioned us to forget who we truly are?

Taking the mask off, or disidentification, is not some form of nihilism but rather the act of reclaiming your original clarity. It is knowing, *I am aware of thoughts, but I am not my thoughts. I experience emotions, but I am not my emotions.* This subtle yet profound realization marks the difference between being consumed by experience and becoming conscious of it. In a world that teaches you to over-identify with roles, trauma, titles, productivity, and even virtue, disidentification offers liberation. It invites you to return to a state of being that existed before conditioning, before the story, and before the name.

Whereas nihilism views life as devoid of meaning, disidentification reveals that meaning doesn't need to be chained to identity. It allows us to participate fully in life without being possessed by it. As the mystic Ramana Maharshi taught, "The 'I' casts off the illusion of 'I' and yet remains as 'I.'"

In other words, an individual's self persists once all the false selves have been shed. This is the Self with a capital S. It's pure awareness, ever-present, and unshaken.

From a psychological standpoint, disidentification reduces what psychologists call "fusion" with mental content. Acceptance and commitment therapy (ACT) teaches us that when we fuse with thoughts like, *I'm a failure*, we act as though they are facts. But when we learn to observe them, *I notice the thought that I'm a failure,* we introduce spaciousness. That space is where freedom lives. It's the difference between being blinded by light and using it to see.

Neurologically, this practice aligns with the capacity of the prefrontal cortex to regulate the limbic system. Mindfulness and metacognitive awareness strengthen this regulatory ability, allowing us to witness emotion without being overtaken by it. The ancient wisdom of the East finds modern confirmation in neuroscience, where we can train the mind to observe itself. This is real and unwavering sovereignty.

Sociologically, however, this is radical. We live in a culture built on overidentification. Of all economic systems, capitalism profits most from you believing you are your body, your job, your pain, and your persona. The more you believe that you lack, the more you consume. The more you believe you are your trauma, the more you disempower your capacity to heal. Disidentification isn't profitable for systems of control, which is why it has often been relegated to monasteries or mysticism, but the modern world is in crisis precisely because this wisdom has been forgotten.

Consider the contrast between Indigenous midwives greeting the spirit of a newborn and modern society greeting a baby with social security numbers, onesies declaring "Future CEO," and questions about college funds. One sees the soul where the other sees a role. One meets the being and the other projects an identity. Our very first moments of socialization in modernity are entangled in projections, status, and utility.

When we disidentify, we don't renounce life but instead engage it more truthfully. It gives us the power to see clearly without trapping ourselves. In practice, it looks like working without becoming the job and loving someone without losing yourself entirely. Even deeper here, when you remember that you are not the content of your mind but the context in which it arises, you gain the power to choose, to move with intention, and to live life without being possessed.

From this newfound clarity, a new human consciousness emerges, one that remembers awareness itself is the ground of being, and from that ground, we build lives rooted in freedom, not fear.

We are trained into our roles. Before we even know who we truly are, we are assigned identities: student, citizen, sinner, believer, patriot. These labels precede our self-discovery, and over time, we learn to perform them. We associate our worth with what our systems reward. In doing so, we mistake the role for the self, achievement for purpose, and survival for fulfillment.

> *"The privilege of a lifetime is to become who you truly are."*
> – Carl Jung

We've inherited a way of life where identity is shaped through institutional affirmation. We are educated to become teachers, lawyers, bankers, and construction workers. But we are not becoming any of those things. We may work in those occupations, but we never needed to "become" anything. We are the Divine: whole, complete, and inherently worthy. Our religion infects us with the fear of God and threatens our descent into hell. But what could be a greater descent into darkness than the loss of your true divine essence? Our government incentivizes allegiance and calls it patriotism. We give up critical thinking and chain our deeply personal ideologies to a political party's policies. We blindly lump all of our beliefs into Democratic or Republican categories. No issues are scrutinized individually. This is sheep herding, not human sovereignty. And as a result, we self-dilute and submit to an identity we are trained to adopt by external mechanisms of control.

To survive in this world, many of us learn early on to wear a mask out of necessity. Simply put, we become what is praised and suppress what is punished. We mold our words, tone, posture, ambition, and even our values to fit the structures around us. We blindly give up agency in our minds and cling to approval and belonging. This is symptomatic of an over identification with illusions.

Over time, all of this creates a subtle but devastating fracture between our inner truth and our outer performance.

Psychological Consequences

This dissonance, between the self we perform and the self we truly are, creates what Carl Jung called the "split self." It is the overt rupture between the soul and our persona. The persona, Jung explained, is the mask we wear to meet the world. It serves a purpose, but when we over-identify with it, when performance becomes mistaken for personality, we grow psychologically fragile, spiritually starved, and emotionally reactive.

So how does this show up in our actions? We may smile while feeling hollow inside. We may succeed outwardly while secretly longing to disappear. We may be surrounded by people and still feel utterly unseen. Long-term denial of authenticity leads to anxiety, depression, emotional exhaustion, and a quiet existential ache we often cannot name.

In this state, we become emotionally dependent on external markers of worth, such as titles, applause, hierarchies, and social proof. We outsource our value to performance metrics, social media likes, grades, promotions, and theological approval.

> *"Care about what other people think and you will always be their prisoner."*
> *– Lao Tzu*

By doing so, we become prisoners of a value system that profits from our insecurity and thrives on our obedience. The more we conform, the more exhausted we become. The more exhausted we become, the more we look outward for relief. This is not a random outcome. It is the design.

Nowhere is this design more visible than in religious systems, where millions are taught to feel wrong simply for existing as they are. Our natural desires are labeled sinful and our curiosity is framed as rebellion. Any doubt is punished; shame is its sacrament, and you are taught to distrust yourself. But don't worry, your religion has the solution. Just give up your autonomy, sovereignty, and critical thinking. This is your salvation.

> *"In every country and in every age, the priest has been hostile to liberty. He is always in alliance with the despot, abetting his abuses in return for protection to his own."*
> – Thomas Jefferson

Sociological Consequences

When a society values conformity over consciousness, it builds institutions that condition identity from the outside in. Degrees, uniforms, and ranks become shorthand for legitimacy. Those without them are silenced, and those with them are rarely questioned.

> *"Those who tell the stories rule society."*
> – Plato

In this framework, whoever controls the narrative controls identity. Religious, academic, medical, and political systems all act as gatekeepers of meaning. Hierarchy is mistaken for order, affiliation is mistaken for truth, and repetition is mistaken for wisdom. Any nuance becomes a threat.

If you question any part of the system, you are branded disloyal, and if you leave the system, you are labeled a failure or an outcast. But these are oftentimes neither. They are strong signs that you have either not been accepted by a deeply sick system or that your internal constitution refuses self-mutilation.

> *"It is no measure of health to be well adjusted to a profoundly sick society."*
> – Jiddu Krishnamurti

No part of this submission cultivates your clarity. It breeds intellectual laziness and emotional conformity, where the goal is simply to belong. Stop for a second. Take a breath and think critically. What has driven you your whole life? What has fueled your aspirations? Where have you sought comfort? If we look deep enough, we see that we have all stopped asking questions and started repeating answers. We defend labels rather than real lived experience. We become fluent in doctrine, but illiterate in truth.

In our culture, original thought is radical, curiosity is dangerous, and trusting your intuition is revolutionary. So what have we produced from this sick dependency on the external? We have cultivated a society of disconnected individuals, cut off not only from ourselves but also from one another.

"Cautious, careful people, always casting about to preserve their reputations... can never bring about a reform. Those who are really in earnest are willing to be anything or nothing in the world's estimation."
– Susan B. Anthony

Physiological Consequences

But it's not just our psyche that suffers.

When we chronically suppress the truth, especially in environments where authenticity feels unsafe, the stress response is activated. Over time, this constant tension burdens the nervous system, elevates cortisol, and increases the risk of chronic health issues such as cardiovascular dysfunction and digestive disorders.

"The body is your subconscious mind, and it speaks through sensations."
– Candace Pert

What the mind hides, the body stores. Let me know if any of these resonate with you: a tight throat, a clenched jaw, shallow breath, an aching back. These are somatic footnotes to suppressed truth. When we cannot cry, the body creates pressure. When we cannot scream, the body holds tension. When we cannot rest, the body eventually collapses.

In a culture that worships productivity over presence, we're taught to override the body's intelligence. We eat meals on industrial schedules that ignore natural hunger. What we now treat as divine doctrine was in fact designed to enforce conformity to industrial rhythms.

Factories needed workers to show up early, work long shifts, and stay synchronized. That demand created the modern meal structure: breakfast before work, lunch at mid-shift, and dinner after. What had once been flexible rhythms tied to the sun and the body were reshaped into a rigid schedule, keeping human life aligned with industrial time.

> *"Illness is not just an effect of the body, but a message from the soul."*
> – Gabor Maté

We sleep by screens instead of the natural cycles of our sacred bodies. We numb pain through alcohol, drugs, and food, when what the pain really asks is that we listen. Yet again, we have structured our lives artificially, from the outside in. There is nothing intuitive about any of it.

To come home to your body is a deeply spiritual act. To honor your needs is a political one.

Not Normal

So what does all of this mean? It means that what we mistakenly perceive as "normal," this life of performance, burnout, and spiritual confusion, is not part of our divine human design. It is institutional design, and it thrives when we forget who we are. It endures through our unquestioned participation.

The true danger lies in our identification with the roles we have assigned to ourselves. We call it being responsible. We call it being realistic. We call it being good. In reality, it's simply a matter of being asleep. It's time to wake up to our reality.

> *"The truth will set you free, but first it will make you miserable."*
> – James A. Garfield

Awakening is about no longer being ruled by these systems. We can't always walk away from the systems we were born into, but we can begin to live within them with sovereignty. We can pause before parroting the script. We can feel where the armor chains the body. We can question the narratives that tell us what to believe, how to behave, and who to be.

The system cannot co-opt the soul unless we forget we have one.

Your evolution begins with remembering. Remembering your balance, your inner authority, and your original sacred design.

Our Meditation

>Who are you when no one is watching?
>Not the name you answer to.
>Not the roles you play.
>Not the image you've spent a lifetime curating.
>
>Beneath all of it there is,
>a pulse that has never wavered,
>a self that has never been lost,
>only covered by stories too small
>to hold your true essence.
>
>You were taught to chase harmony
>like a distant prize,
>to build yourself through
>approval, performance, and perfection.
>
>But what if sovereignty isn't something you achieve?
>What if it's something you remember?
>
>When the noise quiets,
>when the striving pauses,
>there is a soft knowing that arises.

BEFORE WE FORGET

That is your center.
Alive.
Honest.
Aligned with what is real.
Your wounds have shaped you.
Your titles have opened doors.
But none of them will bring you what you are truly seeking.

You are the space
that can hold contradiction
without collapsing.
You are the stillness
that can hear the divine signal
beneath the static.

So ask yourself gently,
Who have I been told to be?
And who am I when I no longer need to perform?

Your identity is your compass,
a way of moving through the world
with integrity,
coherence,
and life itself.

Claim it with what's real,
and honor it with your truth.

Chapter 8
Embracing the Paradox

What are you? A body? A name? A thought? A story? A spark of awareness? You may have glimpsed your boundlessness during moments of awe or silence, yet you have also lived as a singular self, as someone with edges, history, and personal hunger.

You are both. You are the wave and you are the ocean, a fragment and the whole field, a single thread and the entire tapestry of life all at once. This is not a contradiction to be solved; it's a paradox to be embraced. You were born into a unique form; no one else has lived your exact combination of memories, desires, and fears. Your face, your fingerprints, and your voice are unrepeatable expressions of the universe itself.

As a wave, you experience life from a particular angle, carry the wounds and gifts of a single lineage, and walk a distinct path with free will. This individuality is sacred. It is how the whole knows itself in human form. The soul is not trying to erase your uniqueness; it's trying to animate it with truth. However, when we believe we are only the wave, as most of us do, we suffer. Why? Because we sever ourselves from the deeper truth that sustains us. We cling to identity, we fear change, we compare, and we compete. We become obsessed with self-definition.

To honor your wave is to honor your boundaries, your voice, your preferences, and your pain without mistaking any of them for the totality of what you are. Beyond the story, beyond the skin, beyond the roles and thoughts, you are something vast, formless, and eternal. You are the awareness that watches, the space that holds all experiences, and the presence behind the persona.

This is what mystics across every single culture have described. They tell us that we are the sky in which clouds of thought pass, the stillness in which all movement arises, the One who dreams itself into many. When you rest in the field, you feel no urgency to prove, no separation from life, no fear of death. When you anchor yourself in this field, you don't have to earn peace; it simply is. But a mistake many people make is to seek refuge solely in a field that lies beyond their own wave. To do so is to separate yourself from your sacred body.

The ocean, or Source, has never asked you to abandon the wave. We have instructed ourselves to do so. The Divine is asking you to animate yourself with awareness. The spiritual path is the integration of both. You are not here to choose between the small self and the cosmic Self. You are here to live as the meeting point of the two. To live this paradox means letting your uniqueness be a conduit for something universal. When you embrace this paradox you allow yourself to feel your joy and your pain fully while knowing you are not defined by either of them. It means creating art, starting a business, or building a community that carries the imprint of your true essence, as it serves the collective whole. You are both temporary and timeless, finite and formless, the dancer and the dance itself.

A Beautiful Memory

There will be days when you forget, days when the wave feels too small, too wounded, and too loud. Let them come. Embrace their tenderness. Use those days to teach you. There will also be days when you lose all sense of yourself, when the ocean feels too vast to hold, and you feel like you are lost at sea. Let those days be holy.

It's crucial to not cling to either. Come back to your sacred paradox. Come back to your center. You are here to live it consciously. When you hold the paradox, you embody Source itself. The world needs souls who remember they are oceans of infinite intelligence, who are not afraid to show up as imperfect waves. The world needs you. It craves your unique laughter, your imperfect grief, and your deep love that you express through human skin. No matter what anyone else has told you, you were never meant to be only one.

Understanding this paradox in theory is not enough. You need to live it. You need to embody it. This is awakened living. The practice isn't to choose one over the other but to move between them with grace. Gracefully surfing the ocean, honoring the depth of the current beneath you, and letting it guide you on your individual ride.

What follows here are doorways. Each one offers a path to this sacred embrace, where you experience both truths. Let these entry points meet you exactly where you are right now.

Doorways into the Paradox

1. The Inquiry

Find a place where you can find stillness. Somewhere quiet. Somewhere your body doesn't have to perform, and your mind doesn't have to analyze. Here, nothing needs to be achieved. Sit or lie down in a position that feels comfortable and natural. Let your spine lengthen without effort. Let your breath deepen. With each exhale, invite your muscles to remember: *There's nothing to protect right now.* Let your body understand with all of your essence that this moment is safe. Safe enough to let go. Safe enough to listen.

When you feel ready, bring to mind three identities you rely on most. Find the ones that shape how you introduce yourself. The ones you grip when you're unsure of who you are. They may be roles you perform. They may be wounds you've internalized. They may be labels that once earned you love. Name them out loud. With honesty. With tenderness. With respect for the purpose they once served. There is no shame here. There is no judgment. Just recognition.

Then, gently speak this aloud for each one: "I am a [title/identity], and I honor that. But I am not only that."

Say it slowly. Say it like a truth that's ripening. Feel the words pulse through your body. After you've spoken each one, close your eyes. Let the space deepen. When you're ready, ask yourself silently, inwardly, reverently, *Who am I when all identities fall away?*

Don't chase an answer. Don't try to formulate a reply. Ask with the intention to remember and the willingness to feel, rather than the need to define. Let the question sit in the stillness like a candle in the dark. Let the silence around it become sacred. Let the emptiness teach you something your mind has no words for.

What arises may not be language. It may be a subtle shift, a loosening in the chest, a hum in the belly, or a sudden spaciousness. It may feel like nothing, yet it may feel like home.

This is not a performance. This is not a meditation to complete. This is a remembering, a quiet revolution. You are not the stories. You are not the scaffolding. You are what's left when everything else dissolves. That presence, unlabeled, unpolished, and unbound, is enough. Stay here. Breathe here. Let yourself be held in the truth beneath identity. Let yourself be known without needing to be named.

2. The Expression

Your uniqueness is not a detour or some obstacle to overcome. Your uniqueness is not something to fix, flatten, or transcend in the pursuit of being more spiritual. Your uniqueness is not a distraction from the sacred. It is one of its most vibrant expressions. You were not sent here to erase your preferences, your longings, or your voice. You are not meant to be a blank canvas. You are the brushstroke, the color palette, the beautiful pattern, the pulse of life, creating your masterpiece. You are also not here to dissolve into formlessness. The sacred task is to let formlessness move through your unique form. Source does not bypass detail. It does not stifle your integrity. It asks you to enter it, animate it, and let it reveal itself through your actions.

Choose something you love, something that brings you home to yourself, something that dissolves time and awakens breath. It might be writing, cooking, designing, or simply holding a child. Before you begin, pause. Let stillness in. Let your urgency melt away. Close your eyes and gently whisper inwardly, "*Through this act, may the field move through my form. Through my hands, may something sacred come alive. Through my choice, may I remember I was never separate.*"

Then, with your presence and with your openness, let your actions usher in your return. Let your hands become vessels and look at your movement as a quiet ritual. Because it is. Let each motion, each breath, each decision become your offering. Not a gift to an external god in the sky but to the living current of Source already pulsing within you. You aren't reaching now. You are welcoming that current back, you are feeling it, and in doing so, you are honoring both yourself and Source.

This is about remembering who you are, remembering that you are not a separate wave trying to reach the ocean.

So, let the Divine in. Let the dance move through you. Let it make beauty for the sake of beauty itself.

3. The Embodiment
We have been trained to chase the infinite by trying to escape the finite. We seek elevation by abandoning the body, reaching for something higher as if the Divine lives only in the sky, or some untouchable realm. We glorify the light and formlessness, believing that to be spiritual we must rise above our common everyday experiences.

We forget that the Divine lives within every single one of us. The sacred is entrenched within your flesh. It's your DNA. It's woven into your skin, coursing through your blood and breath. Don't be fooled into believing the body is a cage to escape. It is a chalice to honor. It's your doorway to your sacred return.

Anoint yourself. Use your hands with awe. Move slowly, deliberately, as if you're tending to something holy. Why? Because you are. Live the ceremony in your everyday life. Why isn't this considered prayer? Well, because our religious institutions have trained us to disconnect from our true divinity. These institutions have engineered our fragmentation. Take back reality. Take back your truth. It belongs to no one else, not to any institution, not to any job, and certainly not to any system.

Whisper softly, *"My body is not all of me, but it is worthy of love."* Let those words sink beneath the surface. Let them enter the places where shame once poisoned you. Let them reach the parts of you that have been suppressed, overworked, and overruled.

Your body has carried you for your entire life. Honor it once more. It has been your doorway to your joy, your grief, your sight, your taste, and your love. Your body has held your secrets and metabolized your heartbreak. Your body has shown up for you every single day, even when you didn't want to. Your body may not be perfect according to cultural standards, but who cares? To be hypnotized by your physical form, to seek love solely through it, or to obsess over what society feeds you as beauty is just another form of fragmentation. You no longer care about some external measure meant to restrain your consciousness, because now you see the illusion for what it is.

You are miraculous by any measure worth considering.

The sacred is in your stretch marks, your hair, in your perfectly imperfect shape. It pulses through the sacred rhythm of your breath. It reminds you of your connection to the Divine in the heartbeat that sustains you even when you forget to listen. The church, mosque, or temple is not some distant place you must earn access to. You are walking in it. Living in it. You are it.

Let this remembrance undo your diaspora, your exile, or your quest for God. Let this practice end the quiet war you wage between your soul and your form. Let this end your spirit's desire to rise above your body.

Let your embodiment become your truest sign of devotion.

4. The Relationship

Relationships are one of the most sacred and possibly most triggering spaces we can enter. When we step into a real relationship, vulnerable, soul-baring, and unguarded, we don't just meet the other person. We meet ourselves. We come face to face with our unhealed wounds, our unconscious defenses, our inherited expectations, and our deeply rooted fears of being misunderstood, rejected, or unseen.

Within these relationships, it becomes easy, almost instinctual, to collapse into ego, to defend, to interrupt, to explain, to listen only long enough to craft our rebuttal. In doing so, we regress from connection to control. We shape shift from presence to performance. The ego says, *I am right,* but the soul whispers, *I am real, and so are you.*

The paradox of a relationship is that both your truth and the other's truth can coexist. In fact, it can serve as one of the most powerful illustrations of the Divine. Through your interactions, in the space between, you stare straight into the Source field. You are both dancers, and the space you make for the conversation is the Source offering you space to create. The conversation you sanctify is the dance itself.

So, the next time you feel that familiar spike of tension rise in a conversation, especially with someone you love, pause. Take a breath. Push back the identity you have been indoctrinated to accept as who you are. Feel the impulse to protect and then choose to speak from a deeper place. Say, "I see where you're coming from. Here's what's also true for me." This is no longer about performance or purpose for you. It is about tuning into a higher signal that sees all life as beautiful. That understands what it means to truly love.

You may think you're being weak or that you're accepting an uncomfortable compromise. Your ego doesn't want to give in. Resist this urge and show your sacred maturity. It's a maturity that can hold two truths in the same space without needing yours to overshadow the other's. You are honoring two sacred fragments of the human story, saying what is real for each of them within the larger field of shared existence. You are embodying the Divine through this sacred understanding. You are nurturing reciprocity. You are honoring sacred polarity. You are letting the rhythm of life flourish in real time.

In the garden you are tending to, you are opening the space for love to truly flourish.

5. The Mirror
Nature holds this paradox effortlessly. A tree is entirely itself, rooted and reaching, yet entirely part of its ecosystem. It feeds soil, shelters birds, and breathes rhythm with all that surrounds it. A river follows its own course, winding and tumbling, yet it connects every land it touches, threading disparate worlds into one continuous flow. A rock may appear motionless, but it hums with a presence that defies measurement, quiet, grounded, and ancient. None of these elements strive to justify their place. They do not chase relevance. They do not argue for their worth or merit. They are whole. They are integrated. They are belonging itself.

BEFORE WE FORGET

You are no different. Sit beside a tree, a stone, or a stream, and let its silence speak. Let its stillness soften the noise inside you. Let its integrity steady your scattered thoughts. These living, conscious beings laugh at the idea of performance, and in their presence, so will you. Let them remind you of a kind of knowledge that precedes language, and sense a belonging that comes without achievement. Feel the Divine intelligence that asks nothing of you and welcomes all of you. This intelligence hums, "You do not need to be more, only to be yourself," and then quietly whispers, "You are part of everything, just like me."

Let the space between you and the tree, the river, or the stone become a mirror. A mirror that reflects your true essence. Let it show you that you are, simply by being. It will tell you with unwavering sincerity that you are not your resume, your roles, or even your thoughts. Let nature remind you that you are not here to endlessly become more for systems that return only a fraction of what they give. Trust nature in this moment more than yourself. It is here to remind you that you are holy beyond your wildest dreams.

Our Meditation

You are the ocean.
You are the wave.

You are the breath that belongs to no one.

You are stardust wrapped in a body that bruises and heals.
You are nature that has learned to speak.

You are the single face in the mirror
and the countless faces that live within the world.

For too long, you were told to choose.
To cling to the small self or dissolve into the vast one.
To pick a side in a war that you let them create inside of you.

AARON SCOTT

Your sacred truth lives in your ability to hold the paradoxes within,
and those you honor as you live your life.

It lives there,
in the space where the finite and the infinite touch,
where you remember you are not a contradiction.
You are the pulse where the Divine takes a body.

When you honor your paradox,
you pave the way for our evolution.
For our ability to escape the bounds of illusion
that have shaped our reality.

For letting human consciousness
reach its destined potential.
Where we live in truth
with complete knowledge,
with a desire to love above all else.

You are the path.

Chapter 9
Words Shape Reality

The words you speak affect you more than you realize. Every word acts as a compass for your consciousness, orienting your inner experience and determining the terrain of your life. Words generate momentum. They tell your nervous system what to prioritize, teach your mind what to believe, and signal to your body how to respond.

Even the thoughts in your head carry weight. They are active forces, curating your reality moment by moment. Each repeated phrase, whether internal or spoken aloud, shapes your emotions, reinforces certain beliefs, and subtly guides your perception of what is possible.

Your thoughts and your words together establish the architecture of your self-perception. They influence how you relate to your body, to others, to time, and to your own sense of worth.

When you say to yourself, *I have to get this done,* you subtly override your agency, replacing your choice with obligation.

When you tell yourself, *I'm behind,* you collapse your relationship with time and burden your presence with inadequacy.

When you lie to yourself and declare, *I can't handle this,* you create a barrier to your strength rather than reflect your current limits.

These phrases are instructions, frameworks, true energetic blueprints. When you shift your words, your current shifts.

When you assert to yourself, *I choose to focus on this now,* you reclaim your agency.

When you gently remind yourself, *I'm learning what I need to learn,* you create a space that nurtures you.

When you recognize yourself fully and tell yourself, *This may push me, but I am capable,* you affirm both your truth and your resilience.

When you consciously acknowledge the words you choose, you are taking back the wheel from your hijacked car. This isn't about positive thinking. It's about tuning the signal of your inner life so that your choices arise from clarity rather than conditioning.

With this new orientation, your words become an active portal. They are the ground upon which your consciousness walks, and with every phrase, you are either reinforcing the maze or charting a way out.

Speaking as Source

For centuries, we have been fed the story that all of creation is some deterministic machine, governed by an omnipotent God who designs and directs all outcomes. But neuroscience and quantum physics both reveal this delusion and illuminate the true participatory model of our cosmos. It shows us that Source is not a puppeteer pulling strings from above, but the living field through which consciousness flows, responds, and evolves. In reality, Source is the very framework of all existence, the ship itself. And we are not here to be passengers. We are here to be navigators.

Neuroscience tells us that the human brain is not a passive receiver of reality but an active constructor of it. Our perceptions are shaped not just by what is out there, but by what we expect, believe, and attend to. Brain plasticity shows that our neural architecture is continually reshaped by thought, attention, and emotion. We rewire our perception with every story we choose to tell, every belief we update, every word we speak.

BEFORE WE FORGET

The words we choose function like coordinates, subtly directing where our consciousness goes and what our reality becomes. Every phrase we utter reinforces a worldview, signals priorities to the nervous system, and carves grooves in the mind. Say, "I have no choice," and the body contracts. Say, "I am learning to choose," and the system begins to open. Words give form to thought, and energy to perception. They shape our reality.

At the quantum level, this participatory nature deepens. Consciousness does not simply observe a pre-existing world; it interacts with it. Studies show that particles remain in potential until observed, and that waveforms collapse in response to attention. Reality responds to how we engage it, and words are one of the primary tools through which we engage. Every sentence is a selection. Every word is a signal. The tone we use, the metaphors we rely on, the names we give to experience. They are acts of creation.

We have been led to believe that we are directed by the world around us, victims of its design, or those who have architected it. In truth, all of us together have the power to, and actually are, shaping the world around us, in real time, through what we attend to, believe in, and speak into being. Source provides the possibility space, the infinite field in which all choices live. But it doesn't command the direction. It offers the canvas, the colors, the breath of life-force. We are the ones who paint. We are the ones who choose which vision to bring into form. But we have been blinded to our reality for far too long, which has limited our divine artistic potential.

Free will is the mechanism through which divine intelligence fulfills itself. Every thought, every word, every intention creates a ripple in the field. And words are the steering wheel that many forget they are holding. Speak as if you are unworthy, and your body will brace for rejection. Speak as if you are awakening, and your mind begins to open toward it. Over time, your words become the scaffolding of your identity, and your identity becomes the filter through which reality organizes itself.

We are not small beings trapped in a fixed cosmos. We are vast fields of awareness, participating in the unfolding of life. Reality is relational. The future is being authored by us, and words are one of its primary instruments. When we speak with intention, when we choose words that reflect completeness, sovereignty, and empowerment, we begin to write a different kind of world into being.

Our creation did not happen billions of years ago and then cease. Creation never ended. It continues through every sentence, every story, every moment we remember to speak from alignment instead of automation. If we can collectively digest this, we will put on display, for the whole world to see, the real, tangible, everyday alchemy of our own becoming.

The Institutional Voice

Most of us are not speaking with our own voice. We are repeating a language we didn't choose.

Modern life teaches us to speak in system code, a dialect shaped by function, performance, and survival. It arrives subtly, woven into the phrases we hear every day and eventually echoes without question. In the workplace, we talk about deliverables, deadlines, and human resources, as if people are machines with ports and production rates. In school, we absorb terms like "achievement gap," "data-driven instruction," and "underperformance," as if learning is only real if it can be measured, scored, and compared. In medicine, we are translated into cases, noncompliant patients, risk factors, or a collection of symptoms to treat, as if the body is a malfunctioning device.

In daily life, the language has become even more invisible. We say things like, *I should be doing more, I don't have time, I have to keep up,* and *I'm falling behind.* At first, these phrases seem harmless, just the common speech of a busy world, but if we listen closely, we can hear the quiet violence embedded within them. Each sentence carries a worldview, one that assumes time is scarce and must be conquered, that worth is earned through constant productivity, that life is a race with winners and losers, and that there is no space for mystery, slowness, or emotional truth. We stop speaking from the inside out and begin to recite from the outside in.

When we repeat these phrases often enough, they settle in our bones. We begin to hear them in our heads, as beliefs: *I'm not enough, I should be farther along, I'm lazy, I'm behind, I'm too sensitive, I'm always failing to keep up.* These are not reflections of actual reality; they are linguistic residues, artifacts of a culture that forgot how to value interiority. What sounds like self-awareness is often self-abandonment in disguise. What we mistake for motivation is sometimes just internalized surveillance.

We begin to speak to ourselves the way institutions speak to us, through the lens of pressure, utility, and performance. In doing so, we lose touch with something essential. The soul is still present, but it no longer has language, only a quiet ache. It waits behind the metrics, beneath the noise, listening for a sentence that sounds like home.

The most tragic part is that we rarely question any of it because everyone around us is saying the same things, because this is the language we've been given, because the system has naturalized its logic into our mouths. It feels normal. But it's not.

If we are ever to remember, if we are ever to reclaim the fullness of our lives, we must begin by listening carefully and honestly to what we've been saying. To see the scaffolding beneath it. It is only when we see the invisible walls we've built that we can begin to soften them. It's only when we name the borrowed voice that we can begin to hear our own.

Soul Speak

Somewhere deeper, the soul remembers how to speak. Even if we've forgotten. Even if we've been trained out of it. Even if we've spent years translating ourselves into productivity and politeness, into strategy and small talk, and into sentences that make us sound like we belong in a world that doesn't know how to hear us. Beneath all of that, the soul has not gone silent. It has only gone quiet. It waits for a moment of honesty, for enough stillness to finally be heard.

The soul doesn't speak in bullet points. It doesn't speak in deadlines, metrics, or mandates. It doesn't speak in "shoulds," "oughts," or quotas. It speaks in sensations, in symbols, and in seasons. It speaks in the texture of a memory you can't explain. In the ache behind your ribs when you're pretending to be fine. In the resistance that rises before a yes that isn't true. In the grief that arrives without words, yet somehow says everything.

The soul speaks in fragments that feel like poetry. In long pauses and gut instincts. In truths that don't need to be justified because they are felt.

It might say:

> *I'm moving through something.*
> *There's a tenderness here I want to honor.*
> *This doesn't feel aligned, and I don't need to force it.*
> *I want to meet this moment with my whole self.*
> *I don't know the answer, but I trust what's unfolding.*
> *I need to be with this, even if it doesn't make sense yet.*

These aren't gentler phrases of a weak mind. They are the most powerful, because they are the most honest. They tell the whole story, and they do so with deep awareness. They are frames that seek coherence, widen mystery, and that meet the moment completely.

This is how we begin to inhabit ourselves again, as living, responsive beings with texture, timing, and truth. These words restore the possibility of our presence. They return us to nuance, to the sacred complexity of not always knowing. They give us back the right to move through the world without explaining ourselves into exhaustion.

If we can make this shift, we begin drafting a new structure of our lived reality. We will change the very way we exist inside our own lives. We will alter our inner architecture. We will rewrite the unseen instructions we've been following without question. System-speak teaches you how to perform, but soul-speak teaches you how to belong. System-speak keeps you on schedule, but soul-speak brings you into rhythm. System-speak measures your worth, but soul-speak remembers it. When you make this shift, you realign your voice with your being. You reclaim the intimacy between what you say and who you are.

The words you choose are agreements. They declare what kind of world you live in and what kind of presence you are willing to become. When your language changes, your breath changes as well. When your breath changes, your nervous system listens. When your body listens, your life shifts, quietly but unmistakably, toward inner alignment. And suddenly, you are not inside a system. You are inside yourself. You are no longer echoing the world. You are speaking with it. Then something sacred happens. The world begins to speak back.

Every Sentence is a Door

At some point, you begin to notice. Quietly at first, like light shifting through a room you didn't know had windows. You hear yourself say something familiar, something small, habitual, automatic, and suddenly, it echoes differently. You feel a tightening in your chest, a closing in your body, a shrinking in your energy, and you realize that every sentence you speak opens or closes something in you.

Each phrase is a hinge, a threshold, a signal to your nervous system. It either expands or contracts your capacity to be present. It either deepens your breath or cuts it short. It either liberates you or tightens the leash you didn't know you were still wearing.

If you look closely, you'll begin to see that language is where the soul has been waiting all along. It waits with cool confidence beneath the inherited sentences that tell you who to be and how to behave. Beneath the phrases passed down through school, family, culture, and the machinery of institutions that taught you to narrate yourself like a product or a problem. It lives in the space before the sentence. The soul has been waiting patiently for you to remember what you've always known at your deepest level. You don't just speak. You build. You construct reality through language. You imprint the moment with intention or the absence of it.

This is why each sentence is a door, opening you to a deeper alignment or sealing you off from yourself. Each one invites intimacy or reenacts the old fragmentation. Each sentence is a vote for the world you are helping to maintain or the one you are willing to imagine.

The beauty is, you don't have to overhaul your entire vocabulary to change your life. You just have to notice. Begin with one phrase, one moment of pause before repeating the script, one whispered correction: *"I'm overwhelmed"* softens to *"I need space."* *"I can't do this"* becomes *"I'm at my edge."*

"*I don't have time*" becomes "*I'm choosing something else right now.*" These aren't cosmetic shifts. They reshape the blueprint of how you live your life.

Every sentence is a door, and the soul, always listening, walks through whichever ones you choose to open.

Words are Powerful

In many ancient traditions, the word was considered sacred because it was believed to be creative. Language was how the world came into being. To speak was to summon, to call forth, to shape reality through vibration and intent. "In the beginning was the Word" is more than scripture; it is a metaphysical architecture understood across civilizations. The spell, the sound, the breath behind the utterance, these were literal forces of formation. In Egyptian, Hebrew, Vedic, and indigenous cosmologies, language was the essence of life itself.

Even though modern systems would have us believe that language is a passive conveyor of data, the truth is far older and more powerful. Words are formative. They organize energy. They direct attention. When we awaken, we see clearly that every word contains an imprint of the consciousness that created it. When we speak unconsciously, we reinforce inherited frameworks. When we speak with awareness, we become architects of a new world.

This is exactly why totalitarian regimes censor speech before they ever wield force. It's why textbooks are rewritten long before history is. Why marketing campaigns rename oppression as opportunity, and war as peacekeeping. Control begins in the mouth, in what we are allowed to say, and even more importantly, in what we are trained not to say. Words are the subtle terrain where the most devastating forms of soul-removal occur. Words become more powerful than weapons when speech is silenced.

Silencing metastasizes into the strategic dismantling of perception. When people are denied the words to name their pain, their boundaries, or their dissent, they begin to question the validity of their own experience. This is a well-documented tactic of control. Remove the words, and you blur the awareness. Limit expression, and you limit thought.

This is how real manipulation takes root; through the slow erosion of meaning. When public discourse is surveilled, punished, or coerced into compliance, what emerges is confusion. This confusion is another example of disconnection. It is a disconnection from reality. This is why confusion is fertile ground for control. It fragments and confuses us. In the absence of clarity, narratives are no longer questioned. Power is no longer traced. Reality becomes a curated feed rather than a shared truth.

When speech is silenced over large periods of time it starts to reconstruct our collective consciousness. How does it do this? Well it decides what can be known, what can be felt, and what must be forgotten. When speech is constrained, thought becomes narrow. When certain words are off-limits, entire frameworks of reality vanish with them.

To speak freely is, at its core, a cognitive act. It's how we protect psychological sovereignty. It's how we interrupt the programming. It's how we reclaim authorship over what is real, what is possible, and what we refuse to normalize.

Our Meditation

Let this be the quiet beginning of something new.
A turning inward.
A subtle reorientation.
A small act of remembrance.

Use your words to anchor your awakening.

Language can be an essential tool.
Each phrase you choose is a direction.
Each sentence, a seed.

AARON SCOTT

Speak differently, even once today.
Let your language shift by a fraction.
Let one phrase carry the resonance of your truth instead of the echo of your programming.
Say something that feels like you.
You're the essence.

Let it be hesitant.
Let it be imperfect.
Let it be real.

In doing so,
you are reclaiming authority,
you are steering your perception,
you are declaring belief into form.

When you speak from inner clarity, something begins to move.
A pressure softens.
A story loosens.
A sense of sovereignty returns.

What was once buried beneath inherited scripts rises again.
That is alignment.
That is creation.
And it begins here, with how you speak what is true.

Today, with one quiet sentence, you chart a new course.

Part Three
The Threads

Chapter 10
Unleashed

The idea that human nature is fundamentally savage is not the truth. It's a distortion. More precisely, it is a partial truth extracted from extreme moments and then elevated into a worldview. It reduces the fullness of human potential to a single, cynical storyline, and like most distortions, it reflects more about the lens of those who told it than it does about the nature of who we are.

The myth of the savage human has been passed down, justified, and institutionalized for centuries, embedded in the philosophies, religions, and political systems that shaped Western consciousness. Its philosophical roots are often traced to thinkers like Thomas Hobbes, who, in the seventeenth century, famously described the human condition as solitary, poor, nasty, brutish, and short. In his view, without laws and rulers, humanity would collapse into chaos and violence. It was a vision of the human being as inherently dangerous and in need of external restraint.

This view gained traction during the rise of European empires, where the image of the savage was used to justify colonization. Indigenous peoples were framed as less evolved, irrational, and in need of control. We destroyed lineages, stole land, suppressed human beings, and branded it salvation. Christopher Columbus wrote in his journal about the true nature of the Indigenous people he encountered in the Caribbean. In his October 12, 1492 journal entry, he wrote of them, "They do not bear arms, and do not know them, for I showed them a sword, they took it by the edge and cut themselves out of ignorance. They have no iron. Their spears are made of cane... They would make fine servants... With fifty men, we could subjugate them all and make them do whatever we want."

Religious systems added another layer, teaching us that humans are born in sin, flawed from the start, and inherently untrustworthy without divine correction. This narrative built spiritual frameworks on the foundation of unworthiness.

Meanwhile, it's in modern capitalist and militarized cultures that traits like greed, domination, and competition are cultivated, normalized, and even celebrated. These systems shape savage behavior and then point to it as evidence. They say, "This is what people are like," but they forget to ask what kind of human being the system itself produces.

In contrast, science and cross-cultural studies tell a very different story. Anthropology reveals that early human societies were often cooperative, egalitarian, and relational. Violence was usually a response to resource scarcity or the emergence of hierarchy and control.

Neuroscience shows that we are biologically wired for empathy, bonding, and co-regulation. Mirror neurons, oxytocin, and attunement are built-in features of our Divine form. Developmental psychology confirms that infants are born sensitive, morally aware, and deeply responsive. A vast array of indigenous knowledge systems has described humanity as forgetful, not fallen.

So, yes, humans are capable of harm. We can be violent. We can fracture. But we are also capable of grace under pressure, of sacrifice without recognition, and of remembering beauty in the midst of ruin. The belief in a savage human nature is not a law of the universe. It's a lens, and like all lenses, it shapes what we see. It has served the interests of empires, but it has not served the soul.

A more honest view of human nature begins here. We are not inherently savage, and we are not inherently enlightened. We are malleable, patterned, and deeply receptive. We are shaped by our environment, our stories, our traumas, our loves, and our rhythms. When we are given safety, coherence, and truth, we orient toward inner alignment. Our nature isn't the enemy. Our forgetting is.

A Natural Teacher

Every living system on Earth is encoded with spiritual intelligence, a direct, living wisdom that asks nothing of you but presence. No guru is needed. No certificate is required. Just attention. Just breath. Just the willingness to notice.

The garden teaches us to wait. The storm teaches us to release. The mountain teaches us stillness. The seed, buried in darkness, teaches us that transformation often begins in ways that appear like death. Nature is one wild teacher. When we slow down enough to truly observe the Earth, we stop chasing answers and begin to receive them. Nature does not lecture. It doesn't explain or convince. It simply is. Without ego, without arrogance, and without conditioning, it's a master of presence, a keeper of rhythm, and a mirror of the sacred.

When you walk into the forest with genuine presence, you begin to witness yourself. The still pond reveals the calm you didn't know you had. The shifting seasons remind you of your own sacred cycles. The rising sun mirrors your capacity to begin again.

Nature holds up a mirror to every part of your being, body, mind, heart, and soul, and it reflects without agenda. It invites you to remember that you are sacred. There is no judgment in the forest and no standards to meet in the sky. Just being. Just breath. Just the invitation to align with the intelligence that birthed you. When we let the Earth speak, our soul begins to remember its language. In those moments, clarity arises as comforting, calming peace.

We have been taught to fear the wild, but true wildness is not disorder. It's the grandest exhibition of order ever assembled. It puts on display, every day free of charge, a sacred coherence that towers over our soul-crushing mechanistic logic. The forest doesn't grow in straight lines, yet it thrives.

The tide isn't ruled by clocks, yet it returns in perfect rhythm. The bee doesn't analyze flight paths, yet it finds its way. Nothing about the wild is random. It's deeply, intricately intelligent.

We must remember that wisdom is not always neat, and truth does not always arrive as ten-step programs. Real wisdom is seasonal. It spirals. It reveals itself in rhythm, reciprocity, symbols, and regeneration. The soul is cut from the same cloth. It doesn't follow blueprints; it follows sacred intuition.

You are natural. You are part of nature. When you walk with presence in the forest, you aren't escaping reality. You are returning to the greatest expression of it. Nature echoes, "You were never meant to be tamed. You were meant to belong."

And you always have.

Unleashing Consciousness

When we stop building systems centered around manufactured fear and scarcity and begin honoring the truth of who we are, we create conditions for us to unleash our sacred consciousness. In doing so, we awaken and expand. This brings us into the wildness of nature, which has long been mistaken for savage when, in truth, it is deeply ordered, deeply intelligent, and profoundly alive.

To awaken fully, we must unleash our consciousness. We must return to the wisdom that predates language and unlearn the structures that bind our minds and numb our bodies. Unleashing consciousness is about going beneath the noise, the concrete, and the scripts we've memorized, to the place where everything still pulses with the Divine current. To unleash consciousness is to let Source, not institutions, be your teacher, your scripture, and your mirror. Our world has systematized perception, flattened emotion, and domesticated the soul. When we unleash ourselves, we undo that domestication and root ourselves again in something real. In something alive.

In our digital age, we rely on apps and analytics to orient ourselves, but the Earth offers an older, subtler technology, one that speaks in frequency. The rustling of leaves regulates the nervous system. The scent of cedar ignites something within us the mind forgot. The sound of water slows the breath. These are living algorithms designed to tune us back to truth.

Earth is a master frequency field that operates from a far more beautiful and complex code.

Domesticating Consciousness

As we have seen, our minds have been shaped to serve systems that rarely honor life. They are hyper-organized, task-oriented, and quietly colonized by artificial rhythms. Our mind no longer moves with the sun or the seasons, but instead with alarms, calendars, and productivity apps.

Over generations, we've been conditioned to prefer the artificial over the natural. We obsess over our past actions, we worry about future responsibilities, and with all of our mental anguish we remarkably remain disconnected from the present moment. This is all a narrowing domestication of the mind.

We've learned to compress our sacred life-force into bullet points, checklists, and digital calendars. We override our exhaustion with medication, fill our silent moments with distraction, and treat our rest as laziness. We scroll through filtered images of other people's lives while losing touch with the texture of our own. Even nature, our original teacher, has been reduced to a weekend destination or a photo backdrop. We speak of the Earth as if it were separate from us, as if it were somewhere out there, forgetting that it lives in our blood, our breath, and our bones.

This disconnection has become existential. It reshapes how we think, how we move, and how we relate to ourselves and to each other. It severs us from instinct, dulls our inner compass, and fragments our sense of meaning. We become heads without bodies, minds full of information but empty of wonder. We remember our passwords but forget the birthdays of our loved ones. We chase deadlines but abandon our dreams.

This is not a glitch in the system. It is the system itself. One designed to tame the spirit, suppress the wild, and replace inner knowing with external scripts. It rewards compliance, labels exhaustion as ambition, and calls numbness success. It teaches us to conform and compete, and then sells us comfort as freedom.

But the wild in you is not gone. It has only been quieted. It stirs when your breath slows while gazing at the sunset. It flickers when you stop rushing long enough to notice the wind. It whispers when you cry without apology. It asks you to return with eyes wide open. With wonder and excitement.

You reclaim your inner alignment when you trust what pulses beneath the programming. When you recognize that your existence does not need to be justified. When you see clearly that your deepest truths will never come from algorithms, metrics, or authority.

This is remembering. And it needs you to grant it space.

Doorways to Unleash Consciousness

> **1.** Sit with a tree, simply as your presence beside another's. Let go of any need to interpret or extract meaning. Just be near it. Let your body soften under its shade. Let your breath begin to deepen. Feel how the tree's stillness doesn't demand attention but emanates it. Trees teach by frequency. By simply existing, they remind your nervous system what safety feels like.

> **2.** Choose one element of nature and stay with it, undistracted, for ten minutes. A bee moving from flower to flower. A single breeze weaving through the grass. A leaf spinning in a patch of sunlight. At first, your mind may wander. You may feel bored or impatient. Stay anyway. Let your attention stretch beyond the surface. Watch closely and notice how what seemed simple has become intricate, how what seemed static now pulses with life.

> **3.** Notice the unsettling pace that lives inside you. The rushing, the tension, the subtle clench of needing to keep up. Ask yourself gently, *Who taught me this speed? Whose approval am I still chasing?* Let the wild remind you that nothing in nature blooms year-round, that stillness is not laziness, that rest is not failure, and that slow-

ness is not weakness. It is a sacred wisdom. It is sustainability. It's what keeps life flourishing.

Let each moment in nature become a return to life. Let it be a reminder that you are not separate, that you are not behind, that you are not late. Instead, you are part of a vast, intelligent unfolding, and your only task is to listen, belong, and move in rhythm with it all.

Our Meditation

>The Earth is not outside of you.
>The forest is not separate from your mind.
>The wind is not foreign to your breath.
>
>You are not a guest here.
>You are a cell in the body of this world.
>
>The wild within you is not dangerous.
>It is wise.
>It carries the memory of truths the modern world has forgotten.
>
>When you reconnect with the living Earth, you begin to notice something extraordinary.
>Nature moves through you.
>
>The forest has its breath, and so do you.
>The tides have their rhythm, and so does your heart.
>The seasons turn, and something in you turns with them.
>
>To awaken is to remember that you are nature itself.
>Your body is fluid, rhythmic, alive with its own intelligence.

AARON SCOTT

And just as a forest thrives in harmony,
just as rivers find their course through feedback and flow,
so too does the inner landscape of your being.

Breathe as the forest breathes.
Rest as the tides rest.
Rise as the sun rises.

The Earth is your inheritance.
It is your mirror.
It is you.

Chapter 11
The Temple Door

We often approach awakening as a shift in perspective, a reframing of thoughts, a clarity of vision, or a flash of inner knowing. While these cognitive shifts are real and meaningful, they are only part of the process. Insight alone cannot complete the journey. Inspiration without integration leaves the soul floating and the spirit lit, but the body is left behind.

Why? Because if awakening remains only in the realm of your mind, it cannot root itself in your lived experience. It may inspire change, but it will not sustain it. For awakening to become embodied truth, it must pass through the body, specifically through the nervous system.

Your nervous system is the very terrain on which spiritual embodiment unfolds. It's an essential partner. This highly intelligent system serves as the interface between the soul and the soma, between your deepest truths and your daily life. It constantly scans your environment and your inner world, asking one simple question: *Am I safe?*

In every moment, the nervous system filters your experiences through its primal lens. Based on its answer, it determines your state of being. If it perceives safety, you can remain open, connected, and present. If it perceives a threat, you are moved into survival responses like fight, flight, freeze, or fawn.

You can have the most expansive, mystical, life-changing realization, but if your nervous system is dysregulated, you will not be able to hold it. The brilliance of your insight will be eclipsed by the body's need to protect itself. You might shut down emotionally. You might dissociate mentally. You might lash out, numb out, or run away. Why? Because your system doesn't feel safe enough to live it.

Presence becomes impossible when the body is tense and scanning for danger. You cannot stay anchored in love while your physiology is still trying to survive. You cannot embody peace when your entire system is wired for war. This is why so many people feel lost after awakening. The body must feel safe for the soul to stay. Awakening doesn't require more effort; it requires more safety.

When you truly awaken, you walk the path of conscious embodiment. This means tending to your capacity. It means knowing that your nervous system is not a problem to fix. When it's overwhelmed, it needs safety. When it's tight, it needs breath. When it's frozen, it needs warmth and movement. This isn't a call to bypass your nervous system. This is about gently expanding what it can hold.

The depth of your awakening will never exceed the depth of your nervous system's trust.

So, as you continue to grow, remember that the path is not upward into the clouds; it's inward and downward, into the body. It's through the depth of sensation and into the sacred intelligence of your unique form. Root there. Regulate there. The body has never been in the way of awakening. It's the way itself.

Feeling Safe

Your body must feel safe in order to fully awaken. This safety isn't the brittle safety of perfection, certainty, or control. It's not the carefully managed peace you construct by avoiding discomfort or suppressing your truth. It's not the bypassed version of calm that many spiritual teachings mistakenly promote. Rather, it's a deeper, more primal safety, one that lives in the tissues, in the breath, in the space between thoughts. This is a cellular safety born of trust in the moment, in the body, and in life itself.

Presence is the hallmark of awakening, but too often, we are told to "just be present," as if presence were a command we could obey with our willpower, and as if awakening were a purely cognitive shift, available at any time, to anyone, regardless of how dysregulated, exhausted, or guarded their nervous system might be. But presence cannot land in a body that is bracing for impact. It cannot root in a system that is frozen in defense or flooded with unprocessed experience.

Presence is a physiological state. It's what naturally arises when your body finds safety. It's the organic intelligence that returns when your system is regulated and no longer scanning for danger. This means that awakening is about creating an inner environment where fear no longer has to rule over you. It's about creating the conditions in which stillness arises.

In order to live in presence, you must earn the trust of your own body. You must say to your nervous system, *You are safe now. You don't have to be on guard. You don't have to shrink, harden, or disappear*. Only then can you truly awaken, as a living experience. Only then can you open into your truth.

Living Presence

When you find yourself unable to be still, focus, meditate, or "stay in the moment," resist the urge to label yourself as broken or spiritually inadequate. This is not a personal failure or some flaw in your willpower. It's simply a signal. It's a message from within saying, *Something in me does not feel safe yet.*

Rather than pushing harder or shaming yourself with spiritual ideals, pause and ask with compassion, *What part of me doesn't feel safe right now? What is asking to be acknowledged before I can fully arrive? What tenderness is missing from this moment?*

Turn this shift to presence as an act of devotion. In doing so, presence no longer becomes a task with some desired outcome, and transforms into a pathway to a deeper relationship with your self. Welcome it into comfort.

Let your breath slow. Let your body speak. Let your nervous system unwind on its own time. Let stillness be earned through your care. Presence arises when the body feels it's safe enough to soften. It arrives when you have built enough inner trust for you to land fully in yourself. When it becomes a living sensation.

When presence returns, you will recognize it immediately. Your body will exhale. Your chest will loosen. Your mind will quiet without demand. Somewhere deep within, a quiet truth will rise: *Yes. I can be here now.*

Trauma and the Gate

For many of us, our nervous system has learned through repeated, painful experiences to associate our stillness with a threat and our openness with vulnerability. This is adaptation. Your body, in its wisdom, once decided that being fully present was unsafe. You learned that being vigilant was safer than relaxing, and that bracing yourself was wiser than trusting anything or anybody. So, even now, in moments of peace or calm, your body may still hold tension because it remembers what happened the last time it didn't.

This is why certain spiritual teachings you have interacted with, no matter how beautiful or true, felt inaccessible, even triggering. These often leap over the very gate that must be gently approached: the nervous system. Your body does not respond to philosophy. It responds to feeling safe. No amount of conceptual insight will unlock presence if the body perceives the present moment as a threat. To reclaim the body as a sacred vessel for presence, we must meet the trauma stored there with care and gently reintroduce it to safety.

Once regulated, however, the nervous system becomes a doorway into deeper, more stable awareness. A body that feels safe can remain open in intensity. It can feel powerful emotions without drowning in them. It can hold paradox without rushing toward resolution. It can sit in raw, quiet truth without needing to numb, flee, or explain. In this state, you are no longer a container trying to manage everything. Instead, you are a channel, letting life move through you with grace and fluidity.

This is the essence of embodied presence. It's to be fully here, without defense, and to feel everything and remain anchored. So, we must understand that there is no shame in needing safety. You haven't failed nor are you unworthy if you are dysregulated. Use your dysregulation to meet yourself more deeply. In this sacred communion listen, slow down, and rebuild trust with the present moment.

Awakening asks that you turn to your body so completely with attention and care that it becomes spacious enough to hold the Divine current.

Doorways for Integration

The following section is a guide to reconnect with your body and with the present moment. Each doorway is designed to gradually increase your nervous system's capacity to hold presence, allowing you to meet life with greater calm, clarity, and coherence.

Rather than spiritual tricks, these are repatterning tools that help the body remember what safety feels like so that your energy can move freely again.

Your Daily Bodywork Guide

> 1. **Turning to Safety (Morning)**
> **Function:** Waking your body with a sense of safety and spaciousness.
>
> Sit upright or stand by a window. Slowly look around the room or outside. Allow your eyes to rest on 3-5 things that feel pleasant, interesting, or calming.
> Say to yourself, *Right now, I am safe. This is where I am.*
>
> This reminds your body that you're not living yesterday or tomorrow, and that you're not in your trauma story. You're here in the present moment. And it's okay to be here.

2. Awareness Check-In (Anytime)
Function: Returning to your body throughout the day.

Place one hand over your heart and the other on your belly or thigh.

Take a deep breath in through your nose. Exhale through your mouth.
Silently ask yourself, *What do I feel right now?*
No fixing. Just naming.

This builds interoception, your ability to feel and name your inner experience, which is key to your regulation.

3. Coherent Breathing (Anytime)
Function: Resetting your nervous system's rhythm.

Inhale through your nose for 3 seconds.
Exhale through your mouth for 3 seconds.
Repeat for 3–5 minutes.
Count silently. Let each breath lengthen just a little.

This simple breathwork helps to bring your sympathetic (fight/flight) and parasympathetic (rest/repair) systems into balance.

4. Tension Mapping (Anytime)
Function: Learning where your body holds stress and beginning to release it.

Lie down or sit. Bring awareness to your body, from head to toe.
Ask yourself, *Where is there tension? Where is there ease?*
Spend a few breaths with each tense area. Don't force change. Just notice.

This practice helps you befriend your body's language and builds a habit of checking in instead of checking out.

BEFORE WE FORGET

5. Somatic Discharge (Anytime)
Function: Releasing your unresolved defense response.

Stand up. Let your arms hang loose. Shake your wrists and then your arms, shoulders, and legs.
Shake for 1–2 minutes. Let your breath be natural. You can add sound.
Stop. Stand still. Feel your life force underneath.

This is a natural reset used across the animal kingdom. It helps move stress hormones out of your body when your fight/flight energy gets stuck.

6. Vagal Toning with Sound (Anytime)
Function: Activating the body's self-soothing system.

Sit or lie comfortably. Hum softly for 3–5 minutes, or try chanting "*Om*" or singing any gentle sound on the exhale.
Feel the vibration in your chest, throat, or face.

This stimulates your vagus nerve, a key part of your parasympathetic system, signaling that it's safe to relax, digest, and connect.

7. Decompression (End-Of-Day)
Function: Letting go of the accumulated tension of the day.

Before bed, lie down with your knees bent or your legs propped up against a wall.
Close your eyes. Inhale deeply. Exhale with a sigh.
Place a warm compress or your own hand on your belly.
Say inwardly, *I don't need to hold it all.*
Let the ground hold you.

This creates a nervous system signal of closure. It tells your body it's time to downshift and release the day.

AARON SCOTT

Our Meditation

Awakening is not an escape from your body.
It's a return to it.
It's about remembering that your light has always been here.
Inside your chest.
Behind your eyes.
Moving in the rhythm of your breath.

Insight can open the door, but only your body can walk you through it.
Your body will not step where it doesn't feel safe.
Because it is wise.

Safety now is the presence of coherence.
It's the steady hum beneath the waves of change,
the knowing that you can stay with yourself,
no matter what comes.

Your nervous system is the threshold.
The temple door.
It will open when it trusts that you can stand anchored in your life,
without abandoning yourself.

This is why stillness cannot be forced.
Why presence cannot be demanded.
They arrive when the body feels stable again.
They grow in the quiet spaces where you breathe with life,
without rushing to make it different.

So, touch your skin as if it belongs to someone you cherish.
Let your breath drop lower into your belly.
Tell the part of you that is still bracing,
You are safe now.

BEFORE WE FORGET

You need only to build enough trust within yourself,
to stay open when truth arrives.
When that trust takes root,
presence blooms on its own.
And when it blooms,
you discover that the body was never a cage.

It was the doorway all along.

Chapter 12
Parallel Structures

When our systems become too corrupted to be reformed, the sacred response isn't to plead for inclusion or negotiate for scraps of dignity. It's to walk away from the crumbling architecture of empire and to build a new parallel structure entirely.

A parallel structure embodies a new way of being. It dares to make the old system obsolete by living out what the new one makes possible.

The danger, however, is that not all parallel structures are created sacred. Instead of transforming the systems they aim to replace, they end up replicating them. These replicas still operate through fear, hierarchy, or control, only now expressed through different language or dressed in more appealing branding. The surface looks new, but the deeper patterns remain unchanged. To truly guide the new world, we must do something revolutionary. We must build with awareness, from a blueprint rooted in the rhythms of the Divine.

Sacred design embodies spiritual, emotional, and structural coherence. It asks both what we are building and how we are building it. *With what energy? From what awareness? In service of what values?* It calls for systems that regenerate, integrate, and balance for the sake of all ecosystems they touch. They are built to operate in rhythm with the awakened future, unhinged from the trauma of the past.

This is part of the quiet revolution. A revolution that doesn't rage but quietly plants the seeds of an evolved human consciousness. This revolution does not wait for permission or authority. It claims power immediately by building, healing, and organizing in ways that embody care and integrity. We are not mechanics hired to fix an antiquated, stifling machine. We are here to blueprint a more beautiful world and build it beside the crumbling structures. As we do, we shift the center of gravity, making the old rusted husk obsolete.

Let the systems that no longer serve all of humanity fall away. Let the new ones rise, with nourishment. This is how we outgrow the old world. We build something so rooted, so real, and so radiant that people can feel the future in its presence.

The Quiet Architecture

Parallel structures are the quiet architecture of a new world. They are emergent social, economic, and spiritual ecosystems that grow independently of corrupted institutions. They do not seek validation from the systems they transcend. They are not protests pretending to be solutions. They are solutions that emerge through coherent collective action and are sustained by shared values such as truth, justice, care, and interdependence. They are lived expressions of how we relate to one another and the world around us.

These structures do not attract through fear or obligation. They do not manipulate scarcity to create dependency. Instead, they invite life through their presence. When you encounter them, your body recognizes something ancient. Your nervous system relaxes. Something deep inside you says, without force, *This feels right.*

In the realm of education, a conscious and evolved school does not reduce children to data points or standardized measures. It teaches through curiosity, movement, and imagination. Learning follows the rhythms of the body, the Earth, and the soul. In daily life, a regenerative village is not about disconnecting from a power grid. It is about reorganizing life around reciprocity, sovereignty, and care for the land and each other.

A healing collective does not exist to offer cheaper versions of pharmaceutical treatments. It grows from the human need to care and be cared for. Its core aim isn't symptom suppression. Its focus is to bring together science, body-based wisdom, and the sacred. It listens for what truly heals. It responds to what has long been unmet and to what we are just beginning to remember how to ask for.

We aren't looking to recreate a financial system that chases superficial balance by adjusting interest rates and analyzing economic trends. We are looking to create one that finds true balance by meeting real human needs. It's not built around a model of endless growth to offset manufactured inflation, but around balance, sufficiency, and sustainability. It takes the form of transparent exchanges and decentralized systems grounded in trust, care, and mutual contribution.

In the spiritual space, we are not looking for new doctrines or fixed beliefs. The parallel structures we seek in this realm appear in living rooms, under open skies, and in shared community spaces. They are rooted in presence and honesty. No one holds more authority than another. Hierarchy fades away. What remains is a kind of luminous, unguarded humanity meeting itself in the space between.

These structures are not pipe dreams. They are already alive. All over the world, they are quietly working, showing us that what we long for is not something waiting in the future. It is something we are slowly remembering. Each one reminds us that we don't need permission to return to what is true. What we need is the courage to begin again, together, in a new way that aligns with what is real.

Sacred Design

More than aesthetics, sacred design is architecture shaped by care. It encompasses systems, spaces, and structures designed to protect, uplift, and regenerate life. It builds in a way that honors the sacredness of existence itself.

At its center, sacred design asks:

> *Does this system protect life or diminish it?*
> *Does it nourish what it touches or leave it depleted?*
> *Does it bring the soul, the self, and society into harmony or widen the gap between them?*
> *Does it reflect the intelligence of living systems or mimic the cold logic of machines?*

Where conventional design often seeks control and dominance, sacred design is relational. It is attuned to divine pattern and rhythm. It follows the geometry of life, spirals, seeds, waves, seasons. It listens and waits for the right timing. It adapts. It evolves without force. It trusts that growth cannot be rushed and that trying to engineer it stifles what is trying to emerge.

To design in a sacred way is to remember that everything we build carries intention. A curriculum, a governance model, a shared space, a financial system, even a daily practice, each one becomes a vessel for energy. That energy either supports life or fragments it. When we create with presence, design becomes an offering, a quiet act of devotion, and a way of welcoming back the divine rhythm, order, and balance into our everyday lives.

Corrupted systems were not simply built on flawed ideas; they were built on the distorted energetics of domination, separation, scarcity, speed, and hierarchy.

This is why reform often fails. You can tweak the rules, change the branding, or hire more diverse leaders, but if a system's architecture is based on control, it will continue to produce suffering.

Corrupted systems do not reward creativity and inner authority. They reduce people to roles, metrics, and outputs tethered to larger national or global corporate interests. They treat nature as a resource to be stripped in service of unchecked appetites. Most importantly, they silence the soul in the name of order.

Sacred design breaks that pattern by building from a different root system.

BEFORE WE FORGET

As you awaken, the friction with legacy systems becomes more acute. You feel it in your body, in your workplace, in your relationships, and in your inability to go through the motions like before. That dissonance is a signal. It's the soul saying, *It's time to build differently now.*

The Sacred Architect's Checklist

1. Embody Natural Rhythm
Before you build anything, spend time observing nature. Watch how rivers bend, roots spread, and the seasons shift. Let the forms and patterns of the living world guide your choices. Ask yourself what shapes support resilience and flow.

2. Sacred Mapping
Choose a system you interact with often, such as healthcare, education, or work. Reflect on what a sacred alternative might look like. Imagine a version that honors dignity, reciprocity, and care. Then ask yourself what part of that vision you can begin to support or bring into form.

3. Track Your Frequency
Return often to the question: *What am I building from? Is it urgency, fear, or the need to prove something? Or is it clarity, trust, and coherence?* Let your inner state shape the structure you are creating.

4. Invite Others
Share your vision with those you trust. Allow their insights to shape and refine what is emerging. Sacred design grows through relationship, and becomes stronger when tended to by many hands and shaped through shared wisdom. Trust that your vision will resonate because it can be felt by another soul.

Please remember that you were not born just to critique broken things. You were born to remember the pattern of coherence and to build what reflects it. The goal isn't to build it all, just your part with your unique love, clarity and integrity.

We can all see that the old world is falling under its own weight. The new world is rising through your hands.

Build it. Become it.

Exchange that Honors Life

Money itself isn't the problem. It's not inherently corrupt or impure. Money is a symbol, one expression of the values a society chooses to embody. It holds energy and serves as a medium through which we communicate worth. At its best, money serves as a universal language of exchange. The harm doesn't come from the tool itself but from the story we've chosen to tell with it.

For generations, we've been conditioned to see value as something that only comes through the extraction of labor, land, and time. Our systems reward depletion, celebrate accumulation, and treat care and nourishment as privileges rather than basic rights.

But what if we remembered another way to relate to exchange? What if it wasn't governed by fear or dominance but was rooted in mutual thriving? What if our currencies could evolve in tandem with our consciousness?

This is the essence of sacred economics.

Sacred economy doesn't push for policy change, it shifts how we understand energy, value, and relationship. It invites us to reclaim money from our toxic relationship with it and restructure exchange as a sacred act.

Our economy, like all of our systems, is a mirror. It reflects how we relate to time, care, each other, and the living world. In many ways, it is a form of prayer spoken through choices. Every transaction, every offering, every act of giving or receiving carries intention.

The Birth of Economic Disconnection

Modern capitalism is a distorted version of what it could be. It has moved far from its original promise of freedom and opportunity. In its current form, it's centered around separation. Value is measured by what can be extracted or sold by any means necessary. We've learned to separate our love from our labor, our presence from our productivity, and our true well-being from our vision of wealth. In our system, consistent growth is the end goal, and it comes at the expense of people, the Earth, and our deeper sense of purpose.

This distortion didn't come from capitalism alone. It reflects a much older imbalance in our culture. The Sacred Masculine qualities of protection and order were distorted to cold, hard logic and control. The Masculine was overextended and ravaged everything in its path, while the Sacred Feminine qualities of care and relationship were pushed aside. We lost our sacred balance, and without both in the equation, capitalism became overly competitive and extractive. It started running on fear and greed, but its long shadow was forged in conquest, colonization, and systemic erasure.

Colonial Conquest

Capitalism was built on the theft of Indigenous lands and the silencing of Indigenous cultures. From the late fifteenth century onward, European empires swept across the Americas, Africa, Asia, and Oceania, sanctified by papal decrees that named non-Christian lands open for conquest. The Aztec and Inca civilizations were broken by war, disease, and forced assimilation. In North America, the Indian Removal Act tore entire peoples from their homelands. In Australia, terra nullius declared ancient territories empty.

Governance, spirit, and ecological wisdom that had endured for millennia were crushed by missions, schools, and bans. Forests were turned to sugarcane, grasslands to cattle, and mineral-rich mountains to mines of gold and silver. Living worlds became commodities, and their conversion fueled European empires and the rise of global capitalism.

Resource Extraction

Colonial expansion birthed a global economy of extraction. Plantations in the Caribbean and the American South fed Europe with sugar, cotton, and tobacco, exhausting the soils that bore them. Southeast Asia's forests were cut for teak and rubber, while Africa was stripped of palm oil, ivory, and gold.

The Industrial Revolution deepened this hunger. Coal from Wales and northern England powered factories, while colonial networks delivered raw material: Egyptian cotton to British mills, Indian tea to Europe, Caribbean sugar to its tables. Silver from Potosí financed empires, while rubber from the Congo under Leopold II claimed millions of lives through forced labor.

Rivers were dammed, lands drowned, peoples displaced. By the twentieth century, biodiversity was devastated, landscapes polluted, and Indigenous knowledge erased. What once sustained life was turned into wealth, and the living world into profit.

Slavery and Enclosure

The transatlantic slave trade, from the sixteenth to the nineteenth century, tore more than twelve million Africans from their homelands and forced them into the Americas. Enslaved people endured brutal conditions on plantations that produced sugar, cotton, and tobacco, the very goods that fueled European and American wealth. One in five died on the Middle Passage. Profits from slavery built banks, shipping empires, and city infrastructures in London, Liverpool, Amsterdam, and New York. Racial exploitation was woven into the foundations of global capitalism.

At the same time, the enclosure of common lands in Europe stripped shared fields and forests from peasants. What began in the sixteenth century and accelerated in the eighteenth and nineteenth forced millions from subsistence farming into the factories of Manchester and Birmingham. Enclosure severed people from ancestral lands and turned self-sufficient communities into wage laborers bound to markets.

Together, slavery and enclosure transformed both people and land into economic units, entrenching exploitation as a structural feature of the modern world.

Whenever We're Ready

The cold, hard truth is that our modern society sleepwalks in numbness atop a superstructure built on conquest, cemented with stolen lands and the erasure of those who once cared for them.

Our vertical beams rise from human bodies forced into columns of labor, lives reduced to tools to bear our weight. Our horizontal beams stretch across continents, while the joists of enclosure once tore communities from their commons and bound them to markets we still uphold. Our roof is framed from the rafters of extraction, spanning forests, rivers, and mountains. It shelters privilege, while leaving most of life exposed. Our walls hold fast, shutting out the living world, enclosing the human spirit, and silencing the ecosystems we consume. This is the house we live in, the empire we maintain, and it is sustained by our ongoing disregard for life itself.

All of this is the product of a less evolved human consciousness. It has arisen because we have been blinded by the illusion of separateness, and by an immature ego. We must not condemn ourselves. The task now is to evolve and build a future that honors the sanctity of all life.

Our Meditation

> This is our time to evolve
> beyond antiquated ways of thinking and living,
> and awaken.
>
> The truth remains:
> everything in this universe is connected,
> and everything is alive.

AARON SCOTT

Not all of us know it consciously.
Some do.
Many feel it deeply.
Each one of us longs
to bring our sacred life back into bloom.

We can keep sleepwalking,
pushing responsibility onto another generation,
or we can rise now,
for life,
for all that breathes,
for a reality that sustains itself.

A world built through mutual care.

This is our future, waiting to be remembered.

Chapter 13
Awakened Sovereignty

In our passing paradigm, sovereignty was often mistaken for isolation. Autonomy became a kind of armor, worn to protect the individual from the discomfort of dependence. Independence hardened into ideology, raised to the level of unquestioned truth. It taught us that self-reliance was the highest good, even when it came at the cost of our relationships. Somewhere along the way, disconnection was framed as strength.

This distortion has deep historical roots. John Locke and later classical liberals positioned sovereignty in terms of property rights and self-ownership, planting the seeds for capitalist models that rewarded independence, accumulation, and competition. American transcendentalists like Emerson romanticized self-reliance as a spiritual ideal, while rugged individualism became a national ethos. Meanwhile, psychological models in the twentieth century, such as Freud's emphasis on ego development, often pathologized dependency and reinforced the idea that maturity meant detachment. These cultural forces, combined with both individual and collective trauma, led many to equate relational need with weakness and to seek strength through separation.

But awakened sovereignty is about all of us individually coming into coherence with one another.

Sovereignty, in its awakened form, is the ability to remain deeply rooted in our truth while moving fluidly in relationship with the world around us. Our grounded presence tells us, *I am whole in myself, and I am also a part of something greater.*

The soul already knows this. In fact, the soul doesn't know how to speak the language of isolation. It whispers instead that you are a living node in a luminous web, constantly in dialogue, constantly exchanging energy, constantly affected and affecting.

Awakened sovereignty shows up in the collective with self-clarity. It's when you know where you end and where another begins without needing to dominate others, or dilute yourself in the process. It shows itself when you bring your full individual self to the communal table, without performing. Awakened sovereignty invites our intimacy because it remains confident in itself, and glows in the presence of others.

Likewise, to live collectively has nothing to do with homogenization or uniformity. It's when we remember that even our inner selves are inherently relational. You are not only an individual. You are an ecosystem. Your thoughts, language, breath, and nervous system do not arise in isolation. They are shaped by the environments you move through, the relationships you have cultivated, and the invisible field that holds us all.

This moment in human history is asking us to loosen the false binaries. We are being invited into a new kind of power that honors both individuality and participation. This unity is a way of being where each soul stands in its own frequency, clear and distinct, and from that anchoring, we rise together.

This is the evolution of freedom. Born of co-creation, this freedom leads to a world where no one must shrink to belong. Where interdependence is a sacred wisdom to remember. Where we are not here to survive apart but to awaken together.

Fusion or Fragmentation

For generations, the dominant culture has told us we must either conform to the group or stand alone. These extremes have shaped our institutions, our relationships, and our inner lives.

At one end is conformity. The individual self is sacrificed for the promise of belonging. Identity becomes a currency exchanged for inclusion. Authenticity is sacrificed for safety. To survive, you learn to conform. You speak the approved language, adopt the dominant norms, and measure your worth by your ability to fit in. You learn that love and acceptance is conditional. In reality, this is nothing more than safety through submission and illusory belonging disguised as performance.

On the other end is hyper-individualism. In this model, the world is perceived as unsafe, and people are considered untrustworthy. Strength is defined by separation, where freedom warps into avoidance and where sovereignty mutates into isolation. The mantra is "Do it alone." This is autonomy out of fear, not empowerment. Here, your freedom comes at the cost of connection.

Both paradigms are rooted in trauma. Both are survival strategies shaped by a world that did not know how to hold its own coherence. In many spaces, being fully yourself brought rejection, judgment, or threat. The nervous system adapted. It learned that to be loved, you may need to disappear, and to be real, you may need to be alone.

But these are not the only paths available to us.

In the emerging consciousness, a third way is rising. One that is embodied, relational, and spiritually coherent. It is an alternative that honors both the self and the whole. This is the path of interbeing.

Interbeing is a state of mutual presence where boundaries are clear, hearts are open, and individuality is not sacrificed; it is celebrated within a greater web. It is an inner-led connection, where a relationship does not require self-betrayal.

This is what the new world asks of us. In this new paradigm we are not asked to disappear into the group, nor are we asked to intensify disconnection in the name of freedom, but instead to co-create new ways of being together that are rooted in individual truth, in coherence, and in trust.

True belonging invites you to remember who you've always been and bring all of that to the circle.

Tenets of Awakened Sovereignty

Honoring Internal Truth
Awakened sovereignty begins with honoring your individual clarity. It arises from deep listening and finding your true self through inner alignment and integrity. It's the ability to locate your "yes" and your "no" without seeking approval.

Responsible Energy
You recognize that your frequency is your responsibility. You stop blaming others for your discomfort. You pause before projecting. You tend to your own nervous system with care, as if it were sacred ground.

No More Outsourcing
You refuse to outsource your authority to systems, saviors, or groupthink. Awakened sovereignty is not blind allegiance. We see this vividly in political party affiliations, where people defend positions myopically, as if deaf to their own autonomous thinking. This sovereignty doesn't depend on a savior or a guru destined to fly in on a horse or levitate above humanity. It is the decision to remain anchored in your truth, even when belonging asks you to bend. It's the quiet strength of choosing inner alignment, and trusting it will cohere with the sacred as you interact in the living world.

Embracing the Sovereign Paradox
Awakened sovereignty offers a path rooted in genuine freedom. Here you stay steady within yourself while still being moved by what's around you. Here you don't control others, but you stay connected to the flow of life. The paradox of this sovereignty is that

it strengthens your individual self while deepening your ability to relate to those around you.

To build a healthy, balanced, loving world outside ourselves, we must first cultivate these qualities within.

The New Collective

The new collective is a living field defined by coherence. Whereas the old paradigm relied on conformity to create a sense of safety, the new collective welcomes a full spectrum of expressions. Your differences are honored, and here you don't fall into chaos. We welcome varying personal truths and make space for each of them to exist together.

The new collective requires diverse frequencies. No one is demanded to conform, there is no single mold to fit into. You are encouraged to show up as you are, to heal in the ways you need, to create and relate in ways that are true to you. Each of our voices carry its own tone, and each tone contributes to the harmony of the whole.

Here our boundaries operate as instruments of clarity. Our boundaries allow our individual energies to move cleanly and without distortion. All of this makes it possible to stay connected without losing ourselves.

In this coherent nest, our truth arises through presence. It's revealed through authenticity, and ultimately, it's something we uncover together in the shared space between us.

The new collective invites you to ask new questions. What becomes possible when we gather to co-create, not conform? What shifts when connection is prioritized? How much more sacred could our lives become if we allowed ourselves to feel?

Here you are welcomed exactly as you are.

Doorways to Awakened Sovereignty

1. Seek Clarity First
Let your sovereignty choose your collective. Before you join any movement, ideology, or partnership, pause.
Ask yourself:
Does this require me to perform or self-abandon?
Is my truth welcome here, even if it diverges?

2. Speak Honestly Together
Truth is not scary when it's spoken from inner alignment. Practice speaking what's true for you without defense.
Try:
This is what's alive in me right now.
Can I share something that might not be fully formed?
I want to be honest, and I want to stay connected.

3. Sacred Boundary Work
Boundaries protect the quality of connection, not its quantity. They are invitations to healthy relationships.
A sacred boundary says:
I honor myself here.
This is what keeps the field clear.
This is how I stay connected to both myself and to you.

4. Self-Check-In
Each day, practice making decisions from within. Your clarity serves everyone it touches.
Journal:
What does alignment feel like in my body?
Where am I still outsourcing approval?
What do I deeply know that I've been afraid to say?

5. Connection Check

If the collective costs you your sovereignty, it's not yet the future. When in a group or community, ask yourself:
Is this field nourishing me or draining me?
Do I feel more myself after participating?
Is power shared or centralized?

Living Examples

Across the globe, the future is already taking shape. It emerges through quiet experiments in coherent connection. These living demonstrations show what becomes possible when sovereignty is honored with care and integrity.

We see this in decentralized movements where leadership is shared across a network of visionaries. Each person holds a thread of truth, and power is tended to with reverence.

We see it in spiritual communities that nurture inner authority. These circles of remembrance invite each participant to listen inwardly and walk their path with integrity. Everyone belongs within the whole.

We see this in regenerative villages and cooperative models that weave autonomy and interdependence together. Here, sovereignty is experienced as a relationship with the land, with rhythm, and with one another. Freedom arises as a form of rooted belonging.

We see it in creative collaborations where an individual's vision and the collective space are held in sacred balance. Here, the way we work matters as much as what we create, and the space is built to allow for new possibilities to unfold.

These are living laboratories for the future, messy, honest, and evolving. They are imperfect by design, leaving room for growth, feedback, and change.

What they show us is that coherence is something we practice. It becomes real when we create spaces where the individual and the group can grow together, where each person's expression contributes to the evolution of the whole.

Our Meditation

>For generations, we were taught to choose between narrow paths.
>To dissolve into the crowd in search of safety.
>To stand apart in search of freedom.
>To lose ourselves in order to belong.
>To lose belonging in order to keep ourselves.
>Each choice left a fracture in the soul.
>
>Now another way is opening.
>Sovereignty becomes an anchoring that allows us to stay.
>It is the courage to keep the gates of the heart open.
>Belonging is the meeting of distinct frequencies,
>each one clear, each one unique,
>together forming harmony without erasure.
>
>Here we show up in the circle and remember
>that communion awakens us.
>Freedom grows through relationships.
>Relationships deepen through freedom.
>
>The new collective is a living field.
>It grows through connection.
>It flourishes through the intelligence that emerges
>when we move together as one.
>Boundaries bring clarity.
>Difference enriches the whole.
>
>What is asked of you is your presence,
>and the truth that belongs to us all.
>Offered.
>Received.

BEFORE WE FORGET

This is the practice.
This is the rhythm.
This is how the individual self and the whole
remember each other again.

Part Four
The Return

Chapter 14
Living the Frequency

You have already traveled far. Through forgetting and fracture. Through the ache of unraveling. Through crafting the design of a new living world. As we close the arc of our sacred return, a soft hum increases its intensity. We seamlessly merge with the vibration of a song beneath the noise of the world. A pulse that takes its time. A rhythm that does not fracture. We begin to find safety in this steady current of life moving through all things. Every breath, every heartbeat, every quiet moment of presence is part of this sacred rhythmic return.

When we live as a sacred frequency our aim is to become a message through presence, and through our awakened actions. This anchoring rhythm deep within begins to resurface and take back the wheel. We are starting to remember.

We start to feel the frequency that is carried through everything in creation. We start to cohere with the vibrations within trees, rivers, animals, sound, and silence. We start to feel every thought, every breath, every choice, every movement as it radiates a subtle signal into the field. We are able to align with our nervous system, our attention, and our state of being, whether we speak or remain quiet. Long before our words arrive, other people feel us as a transmission. And it is this feeling, this resonance, that we embody when we interact with other living beings in our lives. And as we transmit our sacred signal, we become a tuning fork, gently waking others from their misperceived disconnection.

Rhythm and Resonance

By now, we start to see how life reveals itself through rhythm, through cycles, and through relationships. We begin to feel, with newfound sensitivity, how our breath flows in and out, in the same way light fades and returns. We begin to move and pause as a thread in the greater tapestry that is eternally rising and falling. The Feminine and Masculine energies become an internal relationship we incorporate into our daily consciousness. We begin to live attuned to the sacred expressions of balance, unity, and integrity.

We exit our front doors ready to dance through life with our sacred rhythm. We harness a steadiness that guides us when to yield and when to rise, when to express and when to receive. We begin to embody these sacred gendered polarities, and as we continue to meet them with presence, our lives become more fluid. Our lives become ours to live again, in awakened sovereignty.

We feel the pulse of life speaking through rhythm. We begin to understand how we have been divinely crafted to move in relational balance. Sunrises and sunsets begin to offer more than beautiful visuals; they embolden a sense of belonging to something far more powerful than any human-made system of control could possibly construct. And as we soften in the pace of the tides shifting in and out, we recognize the sacred resonance between one another.

Through our connection to the Divine, we see with calm clarity how we belong to the larger cycles of the seasons. We feel, uniquely, how each season carries an energy that flows through us, as they begin, mature, and fade away. We start to rethink the mandated work schedules we once treated as our beacons of light. They start to fade. They start to offer a darker hue than they used to. We now see that there must be balanced times to act and times to rest. These gentle phases start to offer a clarity that we once ached for. And in that clarity, the mystery of life begins to comfort us. We recognize that as we align with these currents, we have something far more powerful backing us up. Something far more powerful than the anxiety offered through superficial expectations and internal preoccupations to fit in. We trust again, in the Divine, and in doing so, we trust again in ourselves. Each time the mechanized program resurfaces, forcing us out of sync with these movements, we feel the resistance internally more acutely. But now, when we feel the distortion, we smile with calm clarity, knowing we have always had the power to shift. We have always had the ability to experience life with flow and ease. Suddenly, our inner alignment begins to manifest itself. With each encounter, we are brought into greater coherence with the unity of life around us.

Truth, Morality, and Ethics

At the heart of every belief system and inner path lies the essential question: *Am I in alignment with what is true?* This question cannot be answered by analysis alone. It must be felt and lived. Sacred alignment is the coherence between our inner being and our outward actions. We are drawn toward this alignment and long to experience it in the way we live. When we are aligned, our words, choices, and behaviors reflect something greater than ego or social expectation.

Truth is now something we sense in the body, something we recognize in the quiet steadiness it brings. We feel it when it arrives as internal clarity, like a breath reaching all the way down. Honesty becomes a practice of staying close to that feeling, and we rely on it to remain whole. Living this way honors us in the most profound sense.

Morality and ethics are often treated as externally dictated standards, but beneath them lies something deeply intimate. At their core, they ask how we care for our inner alignment and our connection to others. Throughout history, ethics have emerged from both reason and from the need to honor our interdependence. When we embrace this truth, morality is no longer something imposed from the outside. It resonates within, and we see clearly that what we do to another, we do to the whole. Knowing we are part of that whole, the joys and sorrows of others ripple through us as our own.

Sacred alignment restores this understanding. It calls us to act in ways that honor our interconnectedness. When we pause to ask, *Is this action in harmony with what feels deeply right, not just for me but for the collective I belong to?* we begin to live with integrity for life itself. Morality and ethics now become living expressions of self-respect and care for all.

It's shocking to us now how modern societal systems have entrenched the illusion of separateness, fragmenting us from one another and from ourselves. We were taught to protect the individual self, to compete, and to strive alone. We have inherited a deep ideological disconnection. In this soil, fear and distortion have taken root, silencing the quiet inner voice that always sensed something was wrong. Looking back, we see how often we ignored that voice, choosing illusion over truth, and how those small betrayals compounded, slowly wearing us down.

Sacred alignment calls us home. It reminds us that truth, honesty, morality, and ethics are not abstractions but living frequencies of our interbeing. They are the experience of harmony with ourselves, with others, with the Earth, and with the unseen web that holds all things. This too is love. In this place, we no longer live from fear or the need to prove ourselves. We have found a steadier comfort, the deep relief of integrity. And as we awaken to this, our very presence becomes a quiet beacon, inviting others to return to their own alignment.

The Sacred Tuning Fork

A newfound responsibility begins to emerge as we feel how every rhythm of our existence mirrors the movement of the soul. We sense how the soul expands and contracts, how it rests and awakens. We remember the times it hid from life's mystery, and we begin to smile, because we have reunited with it in a new, tangible way. When we honor sacred rhythm, we honor our soul. Living this way brings an unwavering stability and a quiet comfort.

We feel now that when we fell out of rhythm with life, it was the soul that ached, and when we softened back into the natural flow, it was the soul that sighed in recognition. When we look more deeply, we see that the soul never needed to prove, persuade, or perform. We now know that the soul cannot perceive separateness, and that its way of expression is inherently relational.

We realign internally and make space for the soul to reemerge and guide our actions. It feels profoundly empowering to let its resonance shape the path of our lives. We begin to see how powerful we could become as a society if we aligned with this rhythm and built our world in its image. We rest in its strength, knowing it is untouchable by the machine we have sustained. We see clearly now that while artificial intelligence may create the illusion of a soul, our essential nature remains beyond imitation.

As you sink into a chair or rest your head on your pillow, a quiet realization arises within. If people were to awaken to these truths, begin tuning in, and transmit together, it would become clear that we have always held the keys. The systems of illusion to which we once gave our allegiance, and the mental chains that kept us asleep, only seemed to hold power because we never questioned them. We had simply never known another way of being. That changes now.

Transmitting Through Presence

As we reconnect to the world both around us and within ourselves, coherence within the body becomes essential. When we feel a pull toward people who are deeply authentic, we recognize that this too arises from the soul. It reflects the soul's relational nature. When we are in the presence of authenticity, we experience more than another person's truth. We come into contact with a shared rhythm, a belonging that affirms our interconnection. This resonance draws us in through its honesty. In those moments, we recognize that what we seek was never performance. We seek what is real. Our coherence steadies us. Authenticity brings the soul to life. In that awakening, the sacred becomes perceptible, alive in the patterns we embody and the relationships we honor.

As we interact with others and transmit our unique frequency through coherence, our presence becomes deeply felt and clearly perceived, often without words. A person grounded in presence does not need to declare their values because those values are lived. You can sense it in the calm steadiness of someone who listens fully, in the way they move through conflict with clarity and care, and in the quiet confidence of someone who speaks with intention. Such moments leave an imprint. They remind others what it feels like to be attuned, to be seen, and to be real. When your life becomes your message, explanation and defense fall away. You become a quiet transmission of truth. There's no forced effort here, just alignment. Presence speaks more clearly than persuasion. And in that clarity, others begin to remember themselves.

The field is the medium of Source. It's the great expanse of being, the quiet hum beneath all things. It moves through everything without division, holding trees, oceans, stars, and breath in one seamless rhythm. Within this infinite weave, the soul appears deeply connected, as a distinct shimmer in the fabric. The soul is the field shaped in your uniqueness. It carries your rhythm, your wounds, and your voice. It's how life remembers itself through your form. While the field is boundless, the soul has its own texture. It's drawn to certain colors, sounds, stories, and longings. It suffers in its own way and loves with precision. You know it through resonance, in moments when you feel yourself completely and deeply connected to something greater. The soul does not dissolve into the whole or stand apart from it. It expresses itself within it, fully and clearly. You are not here to vanish into unity. You are here to bring your thread to the living weave of existence. In doing so, you don't step outside the field. You give it your unique form. You give it your unique voice. With pride, you allow it to be known.

BEFORE WE FORGET

Our Meditation

Pause.
Let your breath return.
Let the hum beneath your thoughts rise up to meet you.
There is a language spoken in silence,
older than words,
truer than external form.

You are a note within the great song.
You are the pulse that echoes through the living field.
Each breath is a blessing.
Each step is a signal.
Each moment a chance to tune again.

Ask gently:
What am I resonating with?
What does my presence carry into the space around me?
Where do I move in rhythm with life,
and where do I resist the tide?

Sacred frequency is something to remember.
It's the soft return to coherence,
where your inner truth aligns with your outward expression.

In your stillness, there is transmission.
In your coherence, others find their center.
You become a mirror.

There is only participation here.
The field is alive.
It listens for your tone.

Let it be one of tenderness,
of love,
and of your quiet truth that calls others home.

Chapter 15
Embodied Mysticism

Mysticism has often been described as a path of transcendence, a movement away from the world, the body, and the senses in pursuit of a higher, disembodied truth. Many traditional teachings have encouraged seekers to abandon the flesh, suppress desire, and escape the illusion of form in order to reach the Divine. Yet for the embodied mystic, the journey is not about leaving but about entering more fully into the richness of everyday experience. This mystic does not flee the body but descends into it, awake. They learn to hear the whisper of the Divine in both the stillness and in the rhythm of breath, in the ache of longing, and the raw pulse of life moving through the nervous system. They feel the Divine in visions beyond and in the weight of tears, the sense of touch, and the tremble of vulnerability. For them, divinity is woven into sensation itself.

The body was never an obstacle to awakening; it is the altar where awakening occurs, the original sacred text written in nerve endings and fascia. It brings us into *the now* and lets us soak it in. When someone walks the path of embodied mysticism, they realize that presence isn't experienced through thinking it, but rather something to be actually felt. Here we reclaim pleasure, emotion, instinct, and the sacred intelligence of the body. It's an invitation to honor the senses for what they should have always been, as spiritual instruments. With them, we taste and touch with awareness, and we move with devotion. The embodied mystic understands that prayer can be spoken through movement, and that divine union is a full and immediate experience of being here in the present. The Divine lives within, wrapped in muscle and memory, walking our uniquely sacred lived reality, where spirit and form have never been apart. The body is not sinful; its misappropriation by institutional religion is. The body needs to be understood as a beacon for clarity. Here, awakening doesn't require rising above life, but rather falling more deeply in love with it. The light you seek has always lived within, waiting for you to feel it again.

Returning to the Body

The spiritual paths that ask us to turn away from the body have unintentionally deepened pain rather than healed it. When teachings bypass the emotional and physical realities of being human, they can leave wounds unacknowledged and unmet. Our pain is never released by avoiding it. These paths have also fostered shame around pleasure, hunger, and emotion, casting the body's needs as distractions or sins. When they disown the flesh, their spiritual path often becomes fractured. Along this path, spirituality falls victim to another method of fragmentation. It is, in truth, another byproduct of misdirection. Their ideals of purity, detachment, and perfection create visions of enlightenment that deny the messiness of being alive. These unreachable standards sever us from the experiential truths of human existence. It severs us from our actual selves.

True mysticism is the intimate knowing that even in the broken places, the sacred lives. You become humbled when you recognize that the Divine is present in your trembling hands, in your clenched belly, and in the quiver of your voice when truth arrives. When you embody this truth, you remember that pain holds holiness, as something to witness, not flee. Pain is the altar where your deeper compassion is formed. Your desire provides direction as a guide. And when your desire is met consciously, you are no longer overpowered by it. Your breath is more than a physiological function. Breath is a bridge that connects what is conscious and unconscious. It illuminates what is human and what is eternal. Breath is a bridge back to our home.

Senses Are Portals

Sight. Sound. Touch. Taste. Smell. These are sacred instruments of revelation. They are the immediate gateways through which the soul perceives the world. It's no wonder why many of our profane religious institutions immediately attacked these sacred portals. When we have direct access to the true Divine we don't need their stifling dogma and false doctrine. We no longer follow their paths to spiritual disconnection.

When we live in attunement with the senses, they become sacred technologies for integration. They draw spirit into form. They bring presence into perception.

Smell Awakens Memory
A scent can transport you across decades in a single breath. It can summon the presence of an ancestor, unlock a forgotten part of your self, or stir a truth that language cannot structure. Smell is time travel. It offers you a direct recall of your past experiences. It activates the limbic system, known to be the soul's deep archive. It plays a central role in storing and retrieving emotional memories, processing olfactory experiences, and associating meaning with them.

Touch the Present
When you touch something it brings you intimately into the present moment. The softness of fabric or the coldness of ice against your skin remind you that you are here and that you have physical form. Your senses solidify this for you. There is no philosophical proof or scripture that can offer a more direct revelation.

Taste Sparks Devotion
Taste can be an act of devotion when you eat food with presence, gratitude, and reverence for life. Each bite becomes a sacred meeting between the body and the world around you. Here you honor the earth's bounty and the individuals that prepared it. When you slow down to truly savor, taste transforms into a form of

prayer. It becomes a ritual where your nourishment creates real communion with the Earth.

Sound Brings Internal Order
Through vibration, sound alters your brainwave activity, nervous system state, and emotional tone without needing conscious interpretation. Your auditory system is evolutionarily designed to detect subtle shifts in frequency, making sound an immediate and powerful stimulus. It communicates with deeper regions of your brain like the limbic system, influencing memory, mood, and physiological coherence. This makes sound a potent means of accessing states of stillness, emotional release, and alignment.

Sight Is a Prayer
When you gaze with awe, you commune with the world around you and magnify your presence. As you experience beauty through your sight, you witness an external transmission. What you attend to shapes how the world reveals itself, and it invites you into a deeper reciprocity between the observer and the observed. In this way, your sight becomes a prayer of attention that honors the life before you.

Most of us are numbed, overstimulated, but under-embodied. We scroll endlessly, consume quickly, and move unconsciously.

When you re-enter the world with awe, you clear a path to refined sensation. You become more aware, and more deeply appreciate your everyday experiences. Senses can guide you into the present moment. It's important to recognize however that not all stimulation leads to awakening. It's the quality of your presence and not the intensity of your experience that reveals the sacred. When you tune the senses with care, they can become instruments of internal alignment. When you abuse them you run the risk of throwing your entire being out of balance.

Sensory Wisdom

The more you meet life through sensation, the more real your lived spirituality becomes. Your body is always honest. It speaks through feeling before thought can catch up and offers feedback before the mind can form a story. When confusion arises, the body becomes a compass:

> A tight chest may signal protectiveness and a need for care or clarity.
> A soft belly reflects trust and openness.
> Tingling resonates as a call to pay attention.
> Nausea may reveal that a boundary has been crossed, reminding you that *no* is a sacred right.

When you follow this innate wisdom, it's important to remove your inherited shame around sensation and recognize that your body's messages are guides. Movements like crying, trembling, sighing, and yawning are somatic sacraments. They are your body engaging in a sacred release. When you attune to these signals you form a greater connection to the Divine, because it creates a direct and embodied pathway to truth.

Our Meditation

> You don't have to renounce the veil entirely.
> You only have to enter your body with greater alignment.

> The body was never a cage.
> It's a chalice.
> It's where the Divine longs to be tasted, touched, and known.

> Set a path where you honor sensation.
> Where your awakening rises from the bottoms of your feet.

> You were never a soul trapped in a body.
> You are the Divine made sensory.

AARON SCOTT

Spirituality is not about rejecting life,
with all its beauty and mess.
The messiness is the point of it all.

Life was re-synthesized into a performance dictated by inhumane principles.
Living is about failing honestly and learning as you go.
When you root with integrity and open yourself to growth,
you reclaim your true path.
The path designed by your soul.

Disassociation, self-betrayal, and impossible ideals,
disconnect you from your true essence.
You realize your return by leaping back into yourself,
honestly, imperfectly.
Completely.

Chapter 16
The Final Teaching

There comes a point on every path, whether spiritual, intellectual, emotional, or creative, where the pursuit of knowledge must yield to something deeper, not because there's nothing left to learn, but because the essential truth has already been heard, felt, and known. The accumulation of insight must give way to integration. It must now take up residence in the body.

This is the moment when the wisdom you've gathered begins to shape your breath, your posture, and your tone of voice. Embodiment is what happens when a principle is lived. When compassion softens your words in conflict. When peace shows up in your heartbeat during uncertainty. When freedom isn't a mantra but the way your body feels when you walk into a room where you once shrank.

You can quote every sacred text. You can speak eloquently of love, presence, and awakening. But if your nervous system contracts every time reality confronts you, if your energy sharpens when challenged, and if your voice tightens when discussing compassion, then the wisdom has not yet dropped into your body. The teaching remains conceptual and half-baked.

Your embodiment is the final initiation. It is where your wisdom becomes witnessable as coherence and integrity. In a world starved of authenticity, this kind of living truth is the most powerful transmission of all.

Information Overload

We are all overloaded with information. There is no shortage of insight. Teachings flow endlessly from books, podcasts, lectures, apps, and courses. You can download entire lifetimes of wisdom with a swipe. You can quote mystics, decode neuroscience, and diagram the nervous system before breakfast. And yet, something remains untouched.

Integration is rare. Presence is fragile. Embodiment is elusive.

We have confused knowing with becoming and insight with true transformation. Conceptual wisdom cannot keep your heart open when your nervous system is begging to shut down. You can study trauma theory and still abandon yourself the instant an old pattern flares. You can memorize teachings on presence and still dissociate the moment conflict appears. You can recite quotes about love and still armor your heart when love comes in real time.

The distance between what we know and what we live is the sacred terrain of integration. It's the space where practice begins, the kind that humbles and softens you, it's the space that meets you exactly where your insight collapses and says, *This is where we begin again.* Use this distance as a sacred invitation.

Parroting your wisdom is not embodiment; it's metabolizing it. Rehearsed answers, or ideas that resonate with you intellectually, are markedly different from your voice carrying resonance, when your nervous system becomes fluent in safety, or when your presence speaks what your words no longer need to.

Embodied awakening isn't lighting a candle through performance. It's to live the flame with sincerity. And in a cold world seeking warmth, it's your flame that transforms.

Embodiment Moves

When you are embodied, you move with internal fidelity. You feel a coherence between your inner truth and your outer expression. In this sacred space, the desire to legitimize who you are feels irrational.

Embodiment anchors when:

- Your body trusts what your mind believes. There's no split, no internal tug of war between your insight and your actions, between your knowledge and your being.
- Your tone carries the frequency of your words. There's no rehearsal here, no editing for manipulation and impact. Only a lived sincerity.
- Your nervous system can gracefully hold your truths that you teach, even when tested, even when afraid, and especially when nothing around you feels certain.

Embodiment means you no longer have to remind yourself of your embodiment. It's no longer a script. It's your reflex. In particular, it shows in how you show up when no one is watching. Here, the spiritual becomes cellular, and as a result, your healing becomes a body walking through the world, flawed and unshakably real.

Embodied Wisdom

Signs of embodied wisdom are subtle, steady, and often invisible to the outside world. They are felt in your nervous system, your choices, and your capacity to remain real. You stay soft during someone else's reactivity because your softness is grounded and not threatened. You've learned that nervous system regulation is a peace offering to the moment.

You name your needs without apology or demand, trusting that your truth matters and that dignity requires no justification.

- You no longer wait for permission to honor yourself.
- You know when to pause, because of your confident clarity.

- You are tuned into your inner compass rather than reacting from habit.
- You can hold intensity, creating a space for powerful energy without being consumed by it.
- You become a vessel of experience and not a victim of it.

In moments when the world pulls you away, you return to your deep, unwavering breath because you know that embodiment is a devotional rhythm and doesn't reside in a fixed state.

And each time you forget, you slip back into sacred memory. The important takeaway is that this transformation simply makes you more human.

Embodiment is where awakening completes its arc. Your path forward now unfolds through listening. Remaining awake and aware. You begin to organize your life around rhythm, pulse, and flow, as measurable, deeply known truths. The game of life reveals itself as blasphemy. Now, you seek to live in the real world, anchored in sacred truth.

Our Meditation

>There comes a moment when the search quiets.
>Because the truth you have been chasing is no longer out there.
>It's here, pulsing under your skin.
>
>Embodiment begins when wisdom starts breathing through your body.
>When you reclaim peace and freedom as your own.
>
>The world stage reveals itself.
>You stay rooted in honesty.
>Your breath ushers in your truth.

BEFORE WE FORGET

In your daily practices, you return to yourself,
in conflict,
in joy,
in grief,
until truth becomes your reflex.

You touch with care instead of control.
You stand without shrinking.
You let wisdom live in your actions.

We live in a world starved for this kind of truth.

And when you become that living truth,
there's no one left to convince.

You become the flame in a world still chasing candles.

Chapter 17
The Path Ahead

You did not come here to transcend this world, to float above it, untouched by its mess. You did not come to bypass the bruises of being human, to ascend into some imagined light that forgets the daily experience. You came to enter it, to feel the textures of existence brush against your skin. To let the grit of reality polish your soul into remembering. To move through this world with intimacy.

And now you can touch it differently with your sacred hands, with a heart unarmored, with your presence that reverberates across the field.

Every page in this book has been a breadcrumb, left by the part of you that never forgot. Each word is a whisper from your own depths. Each idea is a mirror reflecting your buried knowledge. You were never truly lost, only entangled in roles that were never yours, in stories of shame, separation, and scarcity passed down like heirlooms too heavy to carry.

But these breadcrumbs have been leading you out of fragmentation, where you were taught to split yourself into pieces to be palatable, acceptable, and successful. They have been leading you out of performance, where value was currency and love had terms, and back to a place more ancient than words.

They have been leading you back to a memory of always belonging, a memory etched in your bones and pulsing through your body. This is your revelation. Your breath is the covenant, the original agreement.

> Inhale: *I belong here.*
> Exhale: *I trust life.*
> This rhythm is the ceremony you carry with you always.

Your love is the true technological revolution. Your love carries the original algorithm. The sacred intelligence designed to restore balance. When you love, truly love, you disrupt systems of control. You rewrite the very code of reality.

Your care too is revolutionary because to truly care in a numbed-out world is an act of holy rebellion. When you soften where you were told to harden and protect what cannot speak for itself, you are light amid the darkness.

You are not here to become divine. You already are. Your task is to remember your divinity and let the sacred spill into your daily life. Infuse it into your cooking, your crying, and your commuting. You are here to live from that memory and let it ripple into everything you touch. Every conversation. Every decision. Every silence.

This is the return. It's a return to a devotion that breathes awe into the ordinary. The kind that lights candles for presence. It's a return to a life that feels like you from the inside out.

You are the sacred design. Not random, not extra, not too much. You have been designed with precision, shaped by the Source that dreamed you into form. You are the parallel structure, divine and human. You are the bridge who can translate love into systems.

You are the sanctuary through your presence. People seek your clarity because you've made peace with your own questions.

You are the holy vessel of truth and of new realities. You carry within you what this world has forgotten.

So walk as you are, and let your life become the answer to prayers others have not yet found the words to speak.

BEFORE WE FORGET

Your Becoming

All of the truths you've encountered, through books, heartbreak, stillness, and critical thinking, are frequencies, living, breathing codes humming beneath the surface of thought, waiting for your embodiment.

Now it's time for more contact. Contact with the Earth beneath your feet and the breath rising through your lungs. Embrace the raw, messy, holy reality of this moment.

Let embodiment be your final teacher. Invite it to rewire your nervous system through repetition, stillness, and honesty. Allow it to soften your shoulders when you feel seen as a reminder that healing was never a destination and was always a return.

Trust the wisdom of your body through your gut knowing and your breath's rhythm, to lead you back into the classroom of this present moment.

Look to beauty, real natural beauty, to startle you into presence. Welcome your crooked smile in the mirror after you grieve. Marvel at the softness in another's eyes when they say nothing but ask you to stay. Use this beauty to break you open and reroute you toward what truly matters.

Choose presence as a kind of protest. In this world of monetized attention and speed that whisks you past your own body, presence is a sacred refusal. To anchor there is to say, *I will not be numbed. I will not be rushed. I will not forget that I belong to this moment and this moment belongs to me.*

Turn your currency into your care by allowing your tenderness to serve as a gift in a culture that rewards burnout. Now your compassion and care is your measure of wealth. Invest it into humanity and watch it compound across everyone you come in contact with. The elderly store clerk, the clumsy waiter, the distant gas station attendant. Touch them all with your grace.

Embrace all of these sacred shifts as anchors of your awakening. Trust them to orient your choices across all areas of your life. Now your path begins to breathe again. It lives in the way you hold a gaze without looking at the next person that walks by in the background at a restaurant. It breathes through your carefully crafted homemade cookies, and when you honor yourself with a pause, where before you would have responded out of habit. These small acts ask nothing of you but give you everything you are seeking.

Begin here. In the now. Always now. Because now is the only domain that actually exists. It's the gate that never closes and the only place your soul can fully arrive.

You Are the Portal Now

Everything we once sought, from systems, saviors, doctrines, and distant futures, is now asking to be remembered within you. You are now the portal. There's no more waiting for a better world to arrive. You are no longer hoping that someone more powerful or enlightened will create change. You are the frequency that creates new realities. The world shifts through your choices, your presence, and your care. In fact, you are already reshaping it.

You structure the new economy when you give without expectation of something in return and when you circulate your care instead of fearfully hoarding money. You pave the spiritual path when your actions echo your prayers in your daily life. You become a parallel healing system when your listening becomes medicine for another's soul, and when you make a safe space for others to feel without needing to fix a thing.

Every time you refuse to abandon yourself, you shift the collective consciousness. Every time you move from fear into trust, you open a doorway for others. Please stop thinking you are small. You are powerful. It was the systems of illusion that constricted you. You are not here to be rescued.

The savior lies within you.

BEFORE WE FORGET

To Keepers of the Flame

To the ones who feel.
To the truth seekers.
To those who remembered before they had the words to describe it.
To those who walk into the void.

This is for you.

You are the path home.

You are the sacred frequency of a future that remembers.
You are the evolution.

You've made it here because something deep within you is ready
to rebuild, not escape,
to embody light amid darkness.

You are the evidence
that what's sacred can survive inversion,
that the soul can endure distortion.

So, walk proud.
Speak with presence.
Live as a divine transmission.
Let your presence remind others of what they truly are.

You are here to remember,
to reclaim,
to create what's real
so others can find their truth.

Let this be your legacy:
A life that leaves the world and the future more whole.

Thank you for reading *Before We Forget*.
As a gesture of appreciation, I'm offering some bonus materials
to accompany and uplift you on your journey.
Scan the QR code to access your gifts and deepen your exploration.

Scan the QR Code:

I appreciate your interest in *Before We Forget* and value your feedback,
as it helps me improve future versions.
I would appreciate it if you could leave your invaluable review
on Amazon.com with your feedback.
Thank you!

www.ingramcontent.com/pod-product-compliance
Lightning Source LLC
Chambersburg PA
CBHW030248010526
44107CB00031B/1359/J